THE WORLD'S COLUMBIAN EXPOSITION

THE CHICAGO WORLD'S FAIR
OF 1893

D1227768

THE WORLD'S COLUMBIAN EXPOSITION

THE CHICAGO WORLD'S FAIR OF 1893

Norman Bolotin & Christine Laing

University of Illinois Press

Urbana and Chicago

With thanks to Lu Chapin Flannery
for demanding integrity in
journalism, and for JPB who always
did more than she knew.
$\qquad$ —NPB

For REL,
who always had the right word.
$\qquad$ —CL

First Illinois paperback, 2002
© 1992, 2002 by Norman Bolotin and Christine Laing
All rights reserved
Printed in Canada
p 5 4 3 2

⊗This book is printed on acid-free paper

Library of Congress Cataloging-in-Publication Data

Bolotin, Norman, 1951–
The world's columbian exposition : the Chicago World's Fair of 1893 /
Norman Bolotin and Christine Laing.
p. cm.
Originally published: Washington, D.C. : Preservation Press, c1992.
Includes bibliographical references and index.
ISBN 0-252-07081-X (pbk. : alk. paper)
1. World's Columbian Exposition (1893 : Chicago, Ill.)—History.
I. Laing, Christine. II. Title.
T500.B1B64   2002
907.4'773'11—dc21 2001055644

The University of Illinois Press is a founding member
of the Association of American University Presses.

University of Illinois Press
1325 South Oak Street
Champaign, IL 61820-6903
www.press.uillinois.edu

Designed by Sandra J. Harner, The History Bank, Woodinville, Washington

Contents

Preface

WORLD'S FAIRS HAVE DAZZLED AUDIENCES around the globe for nearly 150 years. Beginning with London's Great Exposition of 1851, some ninety world's extravaganzas have been held, most in the United States, Canada and Europe.

The themes and motives of the fairs are similar: to commemorate a historic event, to educate and entertain, to sell new products, to peer into the future, and, although it's rare, to turn a profit for the sponsors.

Some have been more successful—and memorable—than others. The Paris Exhibition of 1889 was a marvel of engineering achievement with its Eiffel Tower. The 1915 San Francisco gala celebrated the opening of the Panama Canal. The string of fairs in the 1930s, in Chicago, Brussels, San Diego, Dallas, Cleveland, Paris, San Francisco and New York, were remarkable for their elaborate commercial displays and uplifting effect on depressed economies. The Seattle World's Fair of 1962 propelled visitors into the next century.

Even the most obscure have their impassioned fans—the historians, archivists, collectors and lucky ones who attended the expositions of the twentieth century—who rate "their fair" as the best.

But when it comes to pure scope, grandeur and far-reaching legacies, the World's Columbian Exposition of 1893 outshines them all. Twenty-eight million visitors. Buildings stretching a third of a mile long. The world's first Ferris Wheel—with cars the size of buses! The first amusement section ever at a fair. Replicas of a full-size battleship and Columbus' three caravels, which were sailed to the fair from Spain. Architectural impact reaching into the new century. These and the many other highlights of the fair enthralled visitors of the 1890s—and likely would thrill the most sophisticated visitor of today.

The World's Columbian Exposition is not intended to be an all-encompassing chronicle of the fair, an academic treatise or a critical review. We leave that to historians and students of architecture. Our hope is simply to take readers on a fun and fascinating journey back to an event that their grandparents or great-grandparents might have considered the experience of a lifetime. *The World's Columbian Exposition* shares their thrilling experience—if only through imagination.

Today we're bombarded with new technology, and we're certainly exposed through the media, if not first-hand, to foreign peoples and cultures. But imagine the 1893 fairgoer's curiosity at encountering foreign peoples and cultures for the first time; his sense of powerlessness in viewing the explosive technology presented; his pride in seeing all the history and progress of mankind in one place. The world was such a different place!

As authors, we have a passion for first-person histories. When we develop, write and design history books—on the Civil War, the Klondike gold rush or the World's Columbian Exposition—we want to breathe it, understand it, feel it. We want our readers to do the same.

In researching this book we examined hundreds of items: books, guides, pamphlets, catalogs, reports, periodicals, correspondence and personal diaries published during the time of the fair; reference books and articles published during the 100 years after the fair; and artwork, coins, medals, souvenirs and ephemera of all kinds.

As in any reconstruction of an event 100 years later, our most difficult task was determining accurate numbers, names and dates needed to piece together our story. Precise building measurements, spellings of architects' names and dates of events may not be critical in this type of armchair travel, but as long-time journalists we strove for accuracy in details as well as in overall presentation.

Still, we must stress some caveats. Discrepancies abounded in the research material. "Official" records were copious, but accuracy was often suspect. The reporting of the day was not particularly pure; more attention was paid to adjectives and adverbs than to facts. Much weight was also given to competition and the rush to be the first out with a guidebook or pamphlet. As a result, many of the maps and guides—even the "official" ones—and reference books were compiled before the fair opened and therefore contained inaccurate or misleading information, ranging from the number of exhibits to details on the contents and participants.

For one Great Building alone, we found eight different measurements given in twelve reference books. In most cases, we resolved discrepancies by using estimates, taking the most-often cited number or turning to our expert reviewers for confirmation.

There were often several different names used for the buildings. For instance, the Palace of Fine Arts was also "Fine Arts Building," "Art Palace," or "Galleries of Fine Arts." For our purposes we simply selected the name that either appeared on the building or was used most frequently in reference materials—and then used that nomenclature consistently throughout the book.

We also want to note that our descriptions of the architectural styles of the buildings are based on the vocabulary used during the period, rather than contemporary definitions. The Great Buildings, for instance, which were variously described as Italian, French or Roman Renaissance, were actually evocations and eclectic blends of several architectural styles from antiquity and the Renaissance.

Photographs are an important element of *The World's Columbian Exposition*. We have attempted to collect the photos and illustrations that most accurately convey the grandeur, flavor and diversity of the fair. Our only regret is that there were so few interior images—of the exhibits, the eateries and the entertainment—simply because of camera limitations, and, we suspect, photographers' obsession with the beauty of the exteriors (as well as the requirements for official photographers to document the exteriors of the buildings rather than the displays).

In addition to our passion for illustrated history, we have an equally intense love of world's fairs. Both of us grew up in Seattle, Washington, and were lucky enough to attend the 1962 Seattle's World's Fair. As an eleven-year-old, Norm spent much of six months wandering the small fairgrounds with its Century 21 exhibits, both during and after hours, the latter because his father worked there. He was the perfect age to drink it all in, old enough to remember and understand, young enough to be awestruck and overwhelmed by the magnitude. His passion for world's fairs was kindled in the summer of 1962. Because she was several years younger, Chris was not as "hooked" on the fair, but today remembers the sheer joy of riding the "Bubbleator" and the elevator to the top of the Space Needle.

Thirty years later, we both can still taste the food, see the colors and feel the excitement.

Our fascination with the Chicago World's Fair can be traced to the purchase of an aluminum medal in 1979 at a coin show. The beauty of the liberty head and Columbus' landing scene on the coin, still in its original World's Columbian Exposition box, sparked our interest in the collectibles of that fair. Our informal research into the exposition began soon after.

The 500th anniversary of Columbus' voyage to America is a wonderful excuse for a book. But the excitement in developing the book is in being able to share our love of world's fairs and to fire the imaginations of readers with visual and narrative snapshots of the most glorious fair of all time.

Enjoy your journey!

Redmond, Washington
July 1992

Norman Bolotin
Christine Laing

OFFICIAL ORGAN WORLD'S YOUTHS' CONGRESS.

JUNE, 1893. { Only World's Fair Publication having a Bonafide Circulation. } THIS JOURNAL GOES TO 1,500,000 MONTHLY READERS. ESTABLISHED FEBRUARY, 1891. NO. 28.

AUTHENTIC WORLD'S FAIR JOURNAL.

WORLD'S COLUMBIAN EXPOSITION
Illustrated
1492 — 1893
DEVOTED TO THE INTERESTS OF THE COLUMBIAN EXPOSITION, ART AND LITERATURE.

COPYRIGHTED 1893, BY JAMES B. CAMPBELL.   ENTERED AT THE CHICAGO POSTOFFICE AS SECOND-CLASS MATTER.

IN COMMEMORATION OF THE WORLD'S COLUMBIAN EXPOSITION.

AFTER THE FAIR

CAMPBELLS COLUMBIAN JOURNAL

LABOR

ART

COLUMBUS

JUNE 1 ST. 1893

THE UNITED TRIUMPH OF LABOR AND ART.

The Execution and enterprise of **This Publication** Received the **Official Endorsement** of the **World's Columbian National Commission.** AGENTS WANTED.

I

Planning and Building the World's Columbian Exposition

Left: An abundance of guidebooks, maps, newspapers and other aids were published for visitors attending the World's Columbian Exposition. But World's Columbian Exposition Illustrated, *launched in February 1891, was the only official journal to cover the fair from its earliest planning stages through construction and the six-month run of the fair. The publication claimed a readership of 1.5 million.*
Above: One of the more popular souvenir medals from the exposition featured the liberty head on the obverse and a Columbus landing scene on the reverse.

THE IDEA TO CREATE A WORLD'S FAIR commemorating the 400th anniversary of Columbus' voyage to America was conceived not by a single inspiration but by a great many enterprising minds throughout the world. The main motivation was a desire to celebrate one of the most important events in world history. On a more practical level, the huge success of the 1878 and 1889 Paris world's fairs, the latter recognized as the greatest fair of its time, undoubtedly heightened enthusiasm. American proponents also were motivated by the triumphs of the first great fair ever held in the United States, the 1876 Centennial Exposition in Philadelphia.

The Philadelphia fair was considered a major accomplishment, at least in terms of the number of visitors. Although the United States and other countries were still recovering from the severe economic difficulties of the mid-1870s, nearly ten million people journeyed to Philadelphia to view more than 30,000 exhibits. Americans were proud of the fair, but felt that it had only scratched the surface in documenting and displaying the truly phenomenal accomplishments of their young nation. A world's fair would be an ideal opportunity for America to prove both its technological and cultural prowess.

Many sources claimed credit for the idea. The Baltimore *Sun* said it published letters promoting a Columbian world's fair in 1876. A St. Louis newspaper called for "immediate preparation for a national observance" of Columbus' discovery as early as 1882. In the mid-1880s several communities and organizations mounted energetic, but fruitless efforts to give shape and direction to a world's exposition. But it was not until 1888 that the first formal proposal was offered.

In June 1888 a plan originating in Washington, D.C., was proposed in the form of a bill introduced to the U.S. Congress. Burdened with the cumbersome title "A Bill To Provide for a Permanent Exposition of the Three Americas at the National Capital in Honor of the Four Hundredth Anniversary of the Discovery of America," it sought a federal appropriation of $5 million for U.S. participation.

Backers of the bill immediately formed a Board of Promotion. The board began the arduous task of canvassing foreign ministers and diplomats from a variety of Central and South American countries to gauge interest and support.

The bill, however, drew admonitions from other cities, which loudly protested the automatic choice of the nation's capital as the site. And so began a heated competition among major U.S. cities seeking to host the World's Columbian Exposition.

Among the key contenders of St. Louis, Washington, D.C., New York and Chicago, the latter three emerged as the strongest possibilities. Chicago made its bid on the basis of its central location and wealth and enterprise. Washington claimed the right as the first city to move forward with the idea and noted its head start in making preparations. New York simply cited its status as the most populous metropolis in the country with enormous capital and boundless resources.

The three cities made presentations before special House and Senate committees. Although New York was acknowledged as the front runner initially, it soon faced a major stumbling block: It could not put forth a suitable or large enough site. Proponents wanted to transform Central Park into a fair site, but encountered vehement opposition from New Yorkers. Washington, on the other hand, had numerous attractive sites, but eventually lost ground because of its lack of a private resource base and nearly total dependence on public funds.

Chicago It Is!

Chicago had a long list of attributes that ultimately made it the best choice for the fair site. It had a thriving business community and a population of one million. The city was also blessed with 2,000 acres of parks, many with expansive waterfront on Lake Michigan, and all connected by wide boulevards. Nearly half of the acreage was in Jackson and Washington parks alone, which were within a half mile of one another. Further, twenty-four different railroads had terminals in Chicago, creating an elaborate and highly efficient network for transporting people and freight. Exhibitors and developers would present massive freight requirements in both volume and speed. Likewise, the anticipated millions of fairgoers would need easy, affordable transportation from all corners of the country, as well as directly to the site once they arrived in Chicago. Reportedly, the city's steam railroads, steamship lines and excursion boats combined could carry more than two million passengers per eighteen-hour day. Chicago could boast one of the largest and most efficient transportation systems in the country.

Congress was impressed. On February 25, 1890, a joint resolution se-

The man who inspired the fair, Christopher Columbus (top), the one who designed it, Frederick Law Olmsted, and the one who built it, Daniel Burnham.

More than 18,000 tons of iron and steel were used in construction of the Great Buildings. Here, workers and managers from the Edge Moor Bridge Company take a break for the camera before continuing their work erecting the massive steel trusses of the Manufactures and Liberal Arts Building. Note in the foreground the rail track used during construction to deliver building materials to the site. These temporary tracks, along with other temporary storage and housing facilities, were dismantled prior to final landscaping and fair opening.

lected Chicago as the host city. President William Harrison gave his approval on April 28, and the political and organizational wheels began to turn.

Two governing bodies were established. Stockholders of the Chicago corporation that had been formed to promote the city as host met and elected a board of directors and officers. The World's Columbian Commission, consisting of two commissioners from each state and territory appointed by President Harrison, was also formed. The two bodies charged into the mammoth task of organizing the fair, raising funds and selecting the site.

A new race was on. The gates to the largest, most spectacular world's fair ever undertaken were scheduled to open in just two short years.

Financing the Fair

First on the planners' agenda was financing. As required by Congress, Chicago had secured pledges for $5 million in public sponsorship for the exposition. The names of nearly 30,000 individuals and corporations, with pledges varying from one share or $10 to 15,000 shares or $150,000, were listed

In January 1892 the interior of the Mines and Mining Building looked more like an enormous factory with sunlight streaming through its roof than a glorious display hall. Just fifteen months later it would be filled with every gem and mineral known to man.

on the books as subscribers to the capital stock of the corporation formed to manage the fair. A noble start, and certainly proof that the city was eager to support the event; but $5 million was barely one-third of the anticipated $14 million necessary to plan and administer the fair, develop the site and construct the core buildings.

Additional monies would come from a number of sources. The city committed $5 million in bonds. "Receipts from sale of privileges," the licensing and sponsorships that today would bring in tens of millions of dollars, would generate a handsome sum of $1 million.

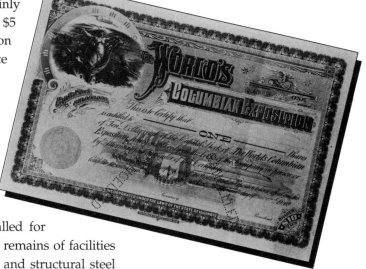

In the initial budget, another half-million dollars would be derived from tearing down the fair! Plans called for dismantling all buildings and selling everything from the remains of facilities and staff uniforms to scrap metal salvaged from exhibits and structural steel used in exhibit halls. In some cases, presales were even made, selling steel from buildings for railroad use.

But the single-largest revenue source would be paid attendance—fair planners projected $7.5 million coming from an anticipated 15 million visitors at 50 cents a head. (Actual attendance soared to 27.5 million, more than 21 million of which was paid, for revenues of approximately $11 million.)

As planning proceeded, the original $14 million budget was quickly doubled to $28 million. Not included in the estimated total was the cost of actual exhibits—nearly 65,000 private, national, state and international displays.

The People Who Made It Happen

Daniel H. Burnham: A Chicagoan, Burnham was named to the seemingly impossible job of chief of construction of the Columbian Exposition. His extensive experience in managing major construction projects had prepared him well. Credited as a man of action and inspiration, he once said, "Make no little plans, they have no magic to stir men's blood." Burnham was masterful in selecting the finest architects, engineers and craftsmen in the world to help execute the grand plan for the fair. His managerial ability, combined with his wide vision as a planner, made the exposition an architectural success.

Colonel George R. Davis: As director general of the exposition, Davis showed his flair for both creative and administrative tasks. He had a long military history, beginning his service in the Civil War, and also served three terms in the U.S. Congress. Davis was instrumental in securing congressional sanction for the exposition and for winning the bid for Chicago to host the fair.

Davis

Harlow N. Higinbotham: Widely recognized for his integrity and strength of character, Higinbotham served in a dual capacity as president of the Exposition Corporation and of the Council of Administration. Drawing on his experience in banking and as a partner in a firm of millionaire merchants, Higinbotham's ambition was to make the stock of the exposition pay dollar for dollar.

Higinbotham

Frederick Law Olmsted: Landscape architect and originator of the general layout for the exposition, Olmsted had devoted his life to the study of parks, forests, zoological and botanical gardens and municipal planning. Among his major designs were the capital grounds in Washington, D.C., Central Park in New York City and public parks in Boston, Montreal and Chicago.

Augustus Saint-Gaudens: Renowned for his creative genius in the world of art, Saint-Gaudens was the principal force behind all sculpture at the exposition. Although previous commitments restricted him to serving primarily as an advisor, Saint-Gaudens chose the sculptors for the main works commissioned by the exposition and oversaw much of the work. His personal artistic contributions included his *Diana* atop the Agricultural Building and the design of the award medal given to winners of various art competitions.

Thomas Wetherell Palmer: A Detroit native and former U.S. senator, the well-liked Palmer was unanimously voted president of the World's Columbian Commission by his fellow commissioners. He was credited with generating much goodwill for the exposition.

Palmer

Bertha Honore Palmer (no relation to Thomas Palmer): As president of the Board of Lady Managers, Mrs. Potter Palmer was a woman of outstanding executive ability, energy and charisma. She was a strong leader with a social conscience. The energy and guiding force behind the Woman's Building, Palmer made her mark on the exposition, adeptly overcoming the gender bias prevalent during the era.

Palmer

The framework for the 348-foot-long, full-size replica of the U.S. battleship
Illinois was actually a foundation. (Inset) Many visitors stepped aboard the
"floating" attraction, unaware that they were on a concrete and wood
structure, not a ship.

Construction methods of the 1890s were labor-intensive, to say the least. Here, a caravan of men and wheelbarrows (still the same basic
model used today) prepare to move dirt and debris during construction of the Palace of Fine Arts.

The Commissary was one of the many temporary structures erected to serve officials and workers during the two years of construction of the World's Columbian Exposition.

Fairest Fair Of All

Planners of the World's Columbian Exposition had the loftiest of goals. The fair was to be bigger in size, more grand in scope and more original in plan than all of its predecessors. It would far surpass all previous fairs in architectural design and beauty. Every square inch, from the most elaborate building to the smallest display, would dazzle the senses and stimulate the mind. In celebrating the progress of mankind, its genius and its treasures, the exposition would bring together all nations and peoples of the world. As one magazine of the period described it, the fair would overflow with "achievements and products of the mind and hand of man such as has never before been presented to mortal vision."

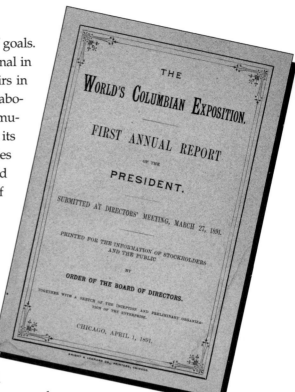

Although fair sponsors most likely didn't realize it at the time, the World's Columbian Exposition would also be the landmark international event that bridged the nineteenth century to the heavily industrialized twentieth century—ushering in some of the most dramatic changes in lifestyle, in the shortest period of time ever experienced by mankind. The fair devoted tremendous space and energy to transportation, a theme given little attention in previous fairs. It was also the most electrified world affair ever held, requiring three times the electricity used to power Chicago on a daily basis and ten times the electrical power used at the 1889 Paris Exposition.

Further, and perhaps most significantly, the fair would have a major and controversial impact on trends in American architecture and urban planning for the next half century.

As planning progressed it became clear that an opening in 1892 would be impossible. Instead, the fairgrounds would be dedicated in the fall of 1892 and the gates would open the following spring.

Goals and purpose established, in the spring of 1890 the massive project of designing and preparing the fair site was the task at hand.

Transforming Jackson Park

There was much controversy surrounding the site. After wasting four months debating possible locations, the Exposition Corporation called in noted landscape architect Frederick Law Olmsted, designer of New York's Central Park. Olmsted and his partner, Henry Codman, reviewed seven sites and quickly decided that the northernmost site on Lake Michigan was the best possibility. Olmsted knew the Jackson Park tract well. Twenty years earlier his firm had developed plans for turning it into an attractive and functional park with quaint lagoons. Unfortunately—or fortunately for fair organizers— Olmsted's plan had never been implemented and the site had been left a flat, uninteresting piece of sandy soil with some scrubby trees. To the untrained eye it was quite unappealing, but to Olmsted it was a clean slate just waiting for his magic.

Olmsted and Codman's masterful plan was to utilize the waters of Lake Michigan as a complementary element to the fair site, dredging a system of

Only the creative eye of an architect such as Frederick Law Olmsted could see the potential in the dreary landscape of Jackson Park in 1891.

navigable waterways and using the dredge material to fill and contour the site with hills and knolls. They envisioned excavating great canals, forming lagoons and islands, and erecting extensive docks, piers, bridges, viaducts and towers. By making the edges of the channels vertical and then filling in behind the walls they would create an effect similar to the canals of Venice.

The duo conferred with Daniel Burnham and John Root, partners in the leading Chicago architectural firm of Burnham & Root, who had extensive experience in managing major construction projects. They liked the plan. A short time later, even before he had made his report to the Exposition Corporation, Olmsted was named consulting architect to the fair and Burnham was named chief of construction.

Olmsted presented his plan to fair organizers and, after some resistance, they agreed: Jackson Park it was!

Like so many elements of the fair, the statuary and building adornment were magnificent. By the fall of 1892 hundreds of artists—probably the largest corps of sculptors and painters ever assembled for a single project—were busy with brush and chisel adorning the buildings of the fair. Chicagoan Francis Millet, a world-renowned artist, directed the painting, and Augustus Saint-Gaudens, perhaps the most distinguished sculptor of the period, supervised the sculpture.

As construction hit its peak roughly one year from opening, the gracefully contoured waterways of Olmsted's plan began to unfold alongside the buildings that lined the shores. The largest Great Building, the 1.3-million-square-foot Manufactures and Liberal Arts Building shown here is nearly finished, awaiting its coat of staff and completion of the roof—a clear span, 368 feet long and 206 feet high.

The 600-acre-plus triangular parcel of land that was to become the World's Columbian Exposition was six miles from downtown Chicago. Transforming the site into a beautiful fairgrounds would be no small undertaking. Two-thirds of the land was described as "a treacherous morass, liable to frequent overflow, traversed by low ridges of sand and bearing oaks and gums of such stunted habit and unshapely form as to add forlornness to the landscape . . . the surface a quagmire, seeming utterly inadequate to bearing the weight of ordinary structures." But Olmsted's plan would overcome the obstacles.

Central to his layout would be a huge lagoon and the Grand Basin, bodies of water around which the fourteen main exhibit buildings, such as the Manufactures and Liberal Arts, Mines and Mining, and Agricultural structures, would be located. These structures would be so magnificent in size and architectural design that they would become known as the "Great Buildings." Three miles of intertwining canals, dotted with elaborate fountains and statuary, would pass by and in some cases encircle the Great Buildings.

In the center of the huge lagoon the sixteen-acre "Wooded Island" would be built. This island, home to a Japanese temple and gardens, would be a peaceful refuge for weary fairgoers.

In addition to the Great Buildings there would be State Buildings, each reflecting the flavor of the sponsoring state or territory. A number of auxiliary buildings and pavilions, such as the Music Hall, Casino, Children's Building and Shoe and Leather Building, would also be included.

This photograph, taken from the Illinois Building just one month before the official dedication ceremonies, shows the expansive, but delicate architecture of the Fisheries Building in the foreground. The building was made of wood, iron, steel, glass and staff. Directly beyond the Fisheries Building are the U.S. Government Building with its brilliant dome, and the sprawling Manufactures and Liberal Arts Building.

Foreign countries would also be well represented. Nearly 100 nations and colonies would participate by erecting buildings or sponsoring exhibits of the inventions and treasures of their homelands. Exposition sponsors were also counting on huge crowds from every part of the world attending the fair; thousands of newspapers worldwide had run public service announcements promoting the fair!

The grounds surrounding the buildings would feature bountiful gardens,

Building Our Great Fair

It is not true that the grounds of our Columbian Exposition in Jackson Park, Chicago, have for months been more interesting than they will be when the Fair is thrown open to the world. And yet they have presented a fascinating study during all the stages of the preparation for the great display; a scene so peculiar that no public exhibition except the completed Fair can exceed it in interest. To have been there and to have watched the construction of the exhibition palaces is to have enjoyed a great surprise and a unique pleasure. The 3,000 spectators on week-days, and the 10,000 who have paid their quarter dollars at the gates on Sundays, will alone be able to boast, when they see the Columbian show itself, that they have enjoyed the full spectacle. They will have seen the earliest and most peculiar exhibit—the mode and progress of construction. It will not dwarf the aggregation of exhibits, but it pales every single one or dozen of them.

It is the custom of the persons concerned in the work to refer back to the time when not a spade had been thrust in the surface of the Fair Grounds, as if that were an interesting period; and truly it is wonderful, now, to see the finished avenues and lawns around the great palaces and the trim-sided lagoons and the orderly beach of Belgian blocks against which the lake's wavelets lick, and to know that here, a year ago, was part jungle, part marsh, and part sandy waste. Of what has been done with the land and water nothing is to me more interesting than the story of the making of the Wooded Island. This island, as all the public must know, is in the main lagoon between the Horticultural Building and the enormous structure for the exploitation of manufactures and liberal arts. It contains sixteen acres, is sparsely wooded, and is designed to be kept rid of all buildings except a superb Japanese temple, and is to be sacred to public comfort. It will be a cool and shady place for visitors to rest upon. One end of it the Japanese will decorate with their peculiar but beautiful flowers and dwarfed trees, and this they have promised to give to Chicago as a lasting memento of their interest in our Exposition. The place was scarcely an island; it was rather a lump of solid sand in a marsh.

Today it is a picturesque islet that anyone would vow had been made by Nature and by her slow processes. The banks slope into the clear water of the lagoon in a very naturally ragged way, with sedge-grass and water-weeds and lilies wading out beyond the edges of the water. Little arms of vegetation and of land reach out here and there between tiny coves and bays, and the general effect is so natural and real that it amazes one to hear that it is not so. Yet the fact is that the island as we see it today is a work of art—of the art of Frederick Law Olmstead [sic] and his partner, the landscape architects. The land was shaped as it is now, and the lilies and grasses and waterplants were put there and made to grow according to a picture or a plan, precisely as the gigantic palaces of the Exposition were first designed upon paper and then executed by mechanics.

Such perfected bits of the Fair Grounds do not speak for themselves, however. One might walk around and over them and never suspect that there was a story to tell concerning them. It is the buildings that are loudly eloquent of their own histories, and that cause repeated exclamations of wonder and delight from all who see them. While they were at their first stage they were less substantial than most skeletons. They looked like mere cobwebs of timber

gently sloping terraces and majestic statuary. The 633 acres of fairgrounds would include 553 in Jackson Park and 80 acres on the Midway Plaisance, originally a one-mile-long, 600-foot-wide strip of wooded land at the edge of the University of Chicago campus, connecting Jackson and Washington parks. The Midway would become home to the exotic amusements and attractions that were not part of the exposition proper—representing the first "side-shows" ever featured at a world's fair.

and iron. Next their sides were latticed with thin wood-work, so that you saw their full dimensions and artistic outlines and proportions, and yet could look right through them as if they were architectural ghosts. Today some are partially at that stage and partially clothed with the staff that is to make them all look like palaces of marble or of ivory. They rise on every hand to great heights with graceful arches and picturesque towers and pinnacles, and already reveal bits of storied entablature, groups of statuary, reaches of decorated frieze, and, in short, strong hints of all that is to compose them.

One cannot be among them, and with the architects and artists who are at work upon them, without feeling that one is upon novel ground . . . that the scene is an artists' festival, and that the entire work is like a materialized dream.
—Julian Ralph, *Chicago and the World's Fair*, 1893

Sculpted from marshland as part of Olmsted's ingenious plan, Wooded Island gave weary fairgoers a much-needed respite from exhibit-viewing. Here, visitors could simply stroll the long walkways and rest on benches for a brief commune with nature. Note that this photograph has been enhanced with illustrated people and boats.

With a general design in place, Chief of Construction Daniel Burnham selected an elite team of the country's finest architects to formulate the ambitious plan for the main exhibit buildings. The committee selected architects for each of the main buildings, except for the Woman's Building. For that building they decided to hold a competition to select a woman architect. Twelve women, remarkably all under the age of twenty-five, submitted sketches. The winner was twenty-one-year-old Sophia Hayden of Boston.

Although each building was designed by a different architect, and each architect was given liberal rein in designing a structure to reflect the theme within, the planning committee had suggested that all be of a classical design, with uniform cornice heights and other measurements. Ultimately, it was also decided that all of the buildings would be the same color, white, to give a unified, pristine appearance to the grounds. (The Transportation Building was the only departure from the white color scheme of the Great Buildings.)

The architects and designers worked feverishly. The spirit of teamwork was remarkable as each strived to contribute to the harmony of the exposition as a whole, rather than to glorify himself through his own building.

Creating the Statuary

There are while I am writing, in early July, 1892, about 10,000 men at work in building the Exposition grounds and buildings. Thousands are laborers who are planting trees, making roads, driving piles, and carting and lifting iron and lumber. But there is one great building full of skilled men led by architects and artists. And in other buildings—even in the most out-of-the-way places—one comes upon painters at work upon frescos, artists illuminating plans with gay colors, sculptors creating beautiful statuary and bass-reliefs [sic], and landscape architects supervising the plans for outdoor displays of foliage and flowers.

The Forestry Building is now the studio of the sculptors' assistants, who are making gigantic enlargements of sculptured models which are to be used on the great buildings. These skilled workmen are mainly Italians, though many are French, and a few, very clever ones, are Americans. Here we see a great deal of the work of Mr. Philip Martiny, of New York, who is

Many buildings were turned into studios where sculptors created heroic statuary out of staff. When completed, this couple would grace the Administration Building.

Ground was broken in January 1891 and the transformation of Jackson Park began. More than one million cubic yards of earth were dredged. More than sixty acres of waterways were created. The entire surface of the ground on which buildings would be erected was raised several feet. The entire lakefront was paved. All of the ground intended to be planted with grass, flowers or shrubbery was covered with loam. An intricate network of streets—effectively enough for a small city—was created. Ninety thousand feet of railway track was laid. An immense pier jutting into Lake Michigan was constructed. The list went on and on.

Nineteenth-century construction techniques were considerably more labor-intensive than today, and creation of the World's Columbian Exposition was no exception. There were hundreds more men with picks and shovels than there were pieces of machinery. At the peak of construction, more than 40,000 skilled workers and laborers had descended on the site.

So impressive was the actual construction that thousands of visitors paid twenty-five cents each to enter the grounds and watch the progress. Spectators could see thousands of laborers, "planting trees, making roads, driving

doing this part of the ornamentation of the Agricultural Building and most of that which is to embellish the Galleries of Fine Arts. The full-relief figures and great medallion busts for that building will be made by Olin Warner, of New York. Carl Bitter is also there at work on the sculptured decoration of the Administration Building . . . and on each side of the doorways. The figures and bass-reliefs [sic] are usually made one-fifth the size they are intended to be, and the after-work of enlarging these is very interesting. The sculptors do this by what is technically called "pointing up." In a word, they take the original figure and determine a number of points upon it as a basis for development. Having put "dividers" upon two points, they keep enlarging third points to the desired distance from the basic points until the figure is the proper size, always beginning from an initial point. Or they make a rough model which assumes the main lines of what they are to produce. This model is usually made of wood built around iron rods and arms, which follow the straight lines of the core of the figure, and serve to keep it strong as with a backbone. They have easily determined the height and width of the statue or figure. The smaller measurements are taken with nails driven in so that their heads are at the right distances from the body. The composition of plaster or staff is then worked upon the figure until it is brought up to these points, and gives the depressions and elevations of the draperies and curves of the subject. . . .

Some of the smaller figures, as of animals and birds, are first made with small bits of lath and whittled pieces of wood. Though they are rude before the composition is

added and worked into shape, they often look very droll, and are frequently strikingly realistic models, like the object to be represented, and yet with angular, unusual lines such as cause us to know that the sheep is to be a sheep, for instance. . . . Some of the giant figures are done in actual staff, where only single figures are wanted and no copies are to be made. The workmen perform their tasks in such cases under the close supervision of the sculptors. Where there are to be duplicates only one is made and that is of plaster. From that a mould will be taken. Gelatin moulds are in use at the Fair Grounds, made largely of glue, and retaining their softness and elasticity, so that when a cast is torn from them their parts yield and pull about and yet return to their original form. This material gives the sculptor a great deal of freedom in his work, and this is preserved in the castings. It is the only process which permits what is called "undercutting," so that the turn or underside of a device, like the lip of a flower or the undercurl of a leaf, may be made with the certainty that it will reproduce finely.

A visit to the Forestry Building shows the workmen at every branch of their operations, and often looking like pygmies as they move among the battalions of gigantic white figures that they have created. Still more like dwarfs do those look who are at work upon the colossal bass-reliefs [sic] which will ornament the arches over some of the palace entrances. Half a dozen men may be perched upon one figure of a woman; one on her shoulder, another on her knees, others working upon her extended arms. Forty or fifty of these sculptors have been busy all summer.

—Julian Ralph, *Chicago and the World's Fair*, 1893

The U.S. Government Building takes shape in 1892. An imposing central dome would soon emerge from the scaffolding in the center of the structure.

piles, and carting and lifting iron and lumber," according to one writer. They could see hundreds of workers literally crawling over the immense frameworks of buildings that climbed hundreds of feet into the sky. They could glimpse a building full of architects and artists adding ornamentation or sculptors creating beautiful statuary and bas-reliefs under the guidance of one of the world's leading sculptors, Augustus Saint-Gaudens, director of sculpture. Or they could watch painters working on frescos, under the direction of Francis Millet, director of decoration. Or landscape architects supervising plans for outdoor displays of foliage and flowers.

Upon completion, the fair became known as the "White City," so named for the gleaming exteriors of the Great Buildings and the ethereal effect they created. Interestingly, the buildings looked as if they were designed to stand the test of time, but they actually were built to last no longer than the six-month run of the fair. Their exteriors were made of "staff," a hard-drying mixture of plaster, cement and hemp that was troweled onto wooden lath. Although the building material was a far cry from the hopes for advances in steel engendered by the 1889 Paris Exposition's Eiffel Tower, the temporary nature of the exteriors did not seem to detract from the brilliance of the architecture or the impressive detail of the ornamentation.

Construction progressed rapidly, but the project had its share of delays caused by weather, materials shortages and transportation problems. Chief of

While construction crews applied staff to building exteriors, legions of sculptors were busy working with staff on interiors and statuary that would adorn the buildings and grounds.

Above: By early 1892, the Administration Building and many of the other Great Buildings had been framed (in iron or steel) and some exterior walls had been completed, ready for an application of staff.

Right: A building material that resembles stucco, staff is a mixture of plaster, cement and fiber that is either contoured over or molded and placed over the wooden lath underlayment forming the exterior walls of a temporary building. The material is as tough as wood and can be bored, sawed and nailed. Staff is still used today for exposition buildings. If painted or treated, it can last many years.

Facts and Figures

Addresses and Conferences: 5,978 addresses were made before audiences numbering more than 700,000 as part of the World's Congress Auxiliary held in conjunction with the fair.

Admission Fee: 50 cents for adults and children.

Attendance: 27.5 million (21 million paid).

Buildings: Fourteen Great Buildings, with a total floor space of 63 million square feet, and some 200 additional buildings. The largest building was the Manufactures and Liberal Arts Building, encompassing 1.3 million square feet or 31.5 acres. There were approximately 200 additional buildings.

Columbian Guard: A force of 2,000 men which provided all police and fire services on the grounds.

Costs: Total cost of the fair (exclusive of private exhibits) was approximately $28 million, including $8 million for the Great Buildings.

Electricity: The exposition required three times the electric lighting power in use in Chicago at the time and ten times that provided for the 1889 Paris Exposition. More than 120,000 incandescent lights and 7,000 arc lights were used at the fair, a great many to illuminate the grounds, fountains and waterways at night.

Foreign Participation: 51 nations and 39 colonies were represented.

Iron and Steel: More than 18,000 tons were used in construction of the Great Buildings.

Landscaping and Site Preparation: Grading and fill work cost $450,000. Dredging cost approximately $500,000, and landscape gardening cost $325,000.

Lumber: More than 75 million board feet were used in construction of the fair buildings.

Public Facilities: 3,000 water closets, 2,000 urinals, 1,500 lavatories

Restaurants: Total capacity of onsite cafes and restaurants was 30,000 people per hour. Each main building had at least one restaurant and many more were sited independently on the grounds and along the Midway.

Sewage and Water: Water plants pumped 64 million gallons per day through 20 miles of water main. The sewage system treated six million gallons per day, similar to a city of 600,000. Sewage was chemically treated and incinerated onsite, with runoff piped into Lake Michigan.

Staff: A composition of plaster, cement and hemp or similar fiber. All of the Great Buildings, many of the State Buildings and most of the statuary were covered or created in the material. Lighter than wood, staff is designed for temporary structures (although if painted regularly it can last several years). More than 30,000 tons were used on fair structures.

State and Territories: 47 states and territories participated.

Waterways: 61 acres of lagoons and waterways ran through the grounds.

Many bas-reliefs were created in staff, including these which encircled the dome of the Administration Building.

The Movable Sidewalk on the Casino Pier was a treat for fairgoers. Shown here under construction, it jutted into Lake Michigan from the southeast corner of the fairgrounds. For 10 cents, the wondrous sidewalk—equipped with chairs—would transport footsore visitors to and from the steamship that ferried them from downtown Chicago.

Construction Burnham was determined to keep construction of all elements of the exposition on schedule. Indeed, he was quite successful. When the gates opened on May 1, 1893, all but a few minor attractions were ready to accommodate the thousands of eager first-day visitors. Perhaps the only major exception was the fair's biggest engineering feat, the crowd-pleaser that would rival the Philadelphia Centennial Fair's spectacular observation tower and the Paris Exposition's famous Eiffel Tower in ingenuity—George Ferris' amazing wheel.

The Biggest Hit

Early in the planning for the fair, Burnham and other organizers had conducted a nationwide contest for ideas on what Americans could build that would outshine the Eiffel Tower as the crowning glory of the exposition. The best of the suggestions, another tower, did not satisfy Burnham. In early 1892

When the fair opened in May 1893 crews were still assembling the massive framework of the giant wheel.

he again solicited ideas: "Mere bigness is not what is wanted," he said. "Something novel, original, daring and unique must be designed and built if American engineers are to retain their prestige and standing."

George Ferris' idea for a huge revolving wheel that would carry forty passengers in each of its thirty-six cars some 264 feet off the ground was at first considered outlandish. Many exposition leaders hinted that Ferris had "wheels in his head." But Ferris persisted, raising from wealthy businessmen and other contributors almost twice the $350,000 needed to eventually gain Burnham's go-ahead.

Ferris' gargantuan creation was not completed until six weeks after the fair opened, but, like many aspects of this fair to end all fairs, it opened the world's eyes to American prowess and ingenuity.

The Dedication

Official counts differ, but somewhere between 100,000 and 500,000 people trekked to the fairgrounds for lavish dedication ceremonies on October 21, 1892, six months before the fair would open. (The festivities had originally been planned for October 12, the recognized anniversary of Columbus' land-

The Statue of the Republic, *the figure that would rise sixty-five feet from a pedestal built in the east end of the Grand Basin, was built in pieces and finished in gold leaf. The head alone, from the chin to the top of the head, was fifteen feet high.*

The biggest hindrance to the finish work at the fair was weather. While foundation work and framing could continue, staff application could not. In January 1892 a patchwork of huge tarps over the Mines and Mining Building provided as much protection as possible from Chicago's notoriously nasty storms.

When the exposition's color department began the task of painting the Great Buildings, they anticipated covering 170 acres of surface with paint or calcimine. To prepare for the work they ordered 50,000 feet of rope, 56 swing-stages, 250 jacks, 500 step-ladders, 5,000 feet of planking, 50,000 pounds of white lead, 5,000 gallons of oil and 500 barrels of whiting. But when they got to the massive Manufactures and Liberal Arts Building and confronted thirteen acres of surface with joists and obstructions, they grew desperate. Their savior was this electric painting machine, which enabled three men to do the former task of twenty. It took ten of these machines and thirty men only six weeks to paint the entire interior of the Manufactures and Liberal Arts Building.

The engraved black and white invitation to the dedication of the buildings of the World's Columbian Exposition

ing.) The celebration started on October 20 in the heart of Chicago, where nearly every street and building was decked out with colorful flags and banners. In a scene reminiscent of a homecoming for victorious soldiers, more than one million people jammed the main thoroughfares and hung from every window and rooftop to witness the huge kick-off parade.

The next day the official dedication ceremonies were held on the fairgrounds amid much pomp and circumstance. A seemingly endless assemblage of fair officials and sponsors, reverends and bishops, governors and generals, ambassadors and foreign heads of state filed onto the platform to address the audience. Though long and most likely tiresome, the hours of orations, invocations, hymns and salutations gave onlookers a privileged glimpse of the wonders they could see in a few short months.

Throngs of spectators clad in formal black lined the walkways of the exposition straining for a glimpse of President Grover Cleveland (seated in first carriage) and fair officials on their inaugural tour of the grounds on Opening Day. Admission to the Opening Day festivities in front of the Administration Building was by ticket only.

Opening Day, May 1, 1893

Opening Day dawned under overcast skies. But the less-than-perfect weather and even the smaller-than-expected crowds didn't dampen the high spirits of the fair officials or onlookers. After the mandatory agenda of invocations and acknowledgments (similar to the dedicatory presentations, but fewer in number and shorter in duration for the sake of the crowds), President Grover Cleveland moved to the center of the platform. He gave a brief congratulatory address and then ceremoniously struck a golden telegrapher's key which activated an electrical circuit to a huge engine in Machinery Hall.

Fountains spewed colorful jets of waters. Flags unfurled. The fair was under way!

II

A Grand Tour of the White City

"The POWER OF THE PEN IS PROVERBIAL, but how inadequate and feeble an instrument it is to describe the picture presented by a bird's eye view of the Exposition Grounds and Buildings. Such beauty, such grace, such coloring! Does there exist to-day, has there ever existed, either on the canvas of the painter or in the brain of the poet, an ideal paradise that will compare with this reality? Spread out beneath him lie more than six hundred acres, upon which has been expended all the wealth of the experience in art and science. The very essence of all that is elegant and unique in landscape gardening, grouped here and there are scores of graceful and imposing edifices, making a magnificent array of structures, which embody the best conceptions of America's greatest architects. Bordering this scene, and adding not a little to it, is Lake Michigan, one of the grandest of inland lakes. There is nothing to add, nothing to wipe out. Could a picture be more perfect?"

—James Wilson Pierce, *Photographic History of the World's Fair*, 1893

Just hours after the gates to the World's Columbian Exposition opened on May 1, 1893, reporters and writers flooded their newspapers with eloquent and detailed descriptions of the long-awaited event. Though many accounts bordered on the poetic, few who saw the fair with their own eyes would dispute the grand portrayals of the world-class extravaganza.

The moment they set foot on the fairgrounds, whether it was stepping off a boat at the Lake Michigan pier entrance, walking through one of the gates directly off Chicago streets, or arriving on one of the many railway lines converging at the exposition terminal, visitors were presented with a panorama of enormous proportions. And yet, from their ground-level vantage, they were seeing but a fraction of the fairgrounds.

Fairgoers were faced with an overwhelming number of choices, whether it was *what* to see at the fair, *how* to see it or *when* to see it. They even had several choices on how to get to the fair.

The most popular route was via water. Those who chose this mode could board a steamer in downtown Chicago for a leisurely and picturesque forty-five-minute cruise to the Casino Pier of the fair. As the steamer left the harbor, clearing the breakwater and heading south, it passed a miles-long collection of warehouses, stately residences, factories and sky-cleaving towers and steeples along the shore and inland.

Then suddenly, almost like a mirage, the White City would appear—at first an indistinguishable mass of gleaming white structures. Slowly, as passengers strained to focus, the largest palaces and towers would single themselves out, creating a stark panorama often likened to a New Jerusalem.

State and Foreign Buildings

As the steamer pulled abreast of the northernmost edge of the fairgrounds (see map on pages 48-49), easing toward the pier on the southern end, passengers would catch a glimpse of the beautiful grounds, the winding lagoons, the spectacular array of buildings, elegant and imposing in their architecture and festive in decoration with hundreds of colorful flags and streamers.

This northern portion of some 100 acres contained the buildings sponsored by states and territories. The New England states were grouped on the lakefront. The buildings of the southern states were grouped toward the center. Midwestern states' headquarters were located in the western portion, and those of the western states started at the fair entrance on 57th Street and formed a semi-circle around the northern edge of the grounds.

Left: The whaleback steamer Columbus *was one of several elegant and streamlined vessels that shuttled fairgoers between the downtown Chicago harbor and the World's Columbian Exposition via Lake Michigan.* **Below:** *This is the view that greeted visitors arriving by steamer. The buildings are, from left, the corner of the Manufactures and Liberal Arts Building, the U.S. Government Building, the Fisheries Building and a collection of distinctive and ornate Foreign Buildings.*

This panorama of State Buildings on the northern end of the fairgrounds shows the diversity of style and size in the structures. The Illinois Building, just to the left of center in the background, dominated the skyline with its huge dome. The California Building, in the style of a Spanish mission, appears at the right in the background. Washington State's building, with its tall flagstaff, could be spotted from a great distance. The water in the foreground is one of the natural ponds of Jackson Park.

Each headquarters was designed to reflect the heritage and character of the state it represented, in architecture, interior design and collection and arrangement of displays. Scanning these grounds, passengers would see everything from the French rococo architecture of the Arkansas Building, designed in tribute to its French settlers, to Virginia's replica of George Washington's Mount Vernon home.

From the lake, passengers most likely couldn't see the two largest state buildings located on the western border of the grounds. But they certainly wouldn't want to miss them once onshore. The California Building, praised as one of the most attractive and unique of the fair's structures, was designed in the style of an old Spanish mission, with Moorish detail. Covering 100,000 square feet, it was second in size only to the Illinois Building. As host of the fair, Illinois was given one of the most favored spots on the fairgrounds, with a view to the south that encompassed nearly one mile over the sparkling lagoon and Great Buildings. In size and architectural pretensions, the Illinois structure certainly ranked among the Great Buildings. It was modeled some-

Above: Still upset at losing the bid to host the fair, New York did not accept the site reserved for its building (above) on the Chicago fairgrounds until the last minute. The state eventually erected one of the most attractive State Buildings. At night it was illuminated by hundreds of lights and its halls resounded with the music of the world's best-loved composers.

Right: Competing with the stunning Palace of Fine Arts on one side and the intriguing Spanish mission-style California Building on the other, the Michigan Building (pictured) and other smaller State Buildings were criticized for their uninspired architecture. However, critics were quieted when crowds numbering 200,000 per day streamed to the state structures. On Michigan's spacious porch weary families could eat a leisurely meal, and inside, great halls could be reserved for evening parties.

what after the state capitol in Springfield and featured exquisite carvings and statuary. It cost $250,000 and contained nearly four acres of main floor and galleries.

In the center of the area containing the State Buildings was the North Pond, the northernmost body of water from which began a labyrinth of waterways. Fronting the pond was the first of the Great Buildings, the Fine Arts Building or "Palace of Fine Arts," as it was most often called. Designed by Charles B. Atwood of Chicago, the generally "Roman-style" oblong building featured a huge nave and lighted transept 100 feet wide by 70 feet high. In the center was an enormous dome topped by a colossal statue, *Victory*, a figure poised upon a globe with outstretched arms offering laurel wreaths. To protect its priceless displays, the building was constructed with fire-proof materials. The main walls were made of solid brick, covered with staff, the hard-drying coating of cement, plaster and fiber used on most of the buildings and statues, and colored to give the appearance of light gray stone. The roof, floors and outside galleries, which formed a continuous promenade around the entire building, were made of iron. The grounds were adorned with statues of he-

Fairgoers approached the south porch of the Palace of Fine Arts by water. This building is the only structure of the World's Columbian Exposition still standing. Today, it is the Museum of Science and Industry.

The whimsical Swedish Building, modeled after the country's churches and castles of the sixteenth century, was built in Sweden and shipped to the United States in pieces.

Sculpted by Mary Lawrence, this statue of Columbus, which graced the eastern entrance to the Administration Building, was one of many tributes to the great explorer.

roic and life-size proportions. The numerous interior galleries featured sculpture and paintings from the United States and foreign countries. Works were both juried and unjuried, primarily from contemporary artists. A mile of hanging space was allocated for paintings due to the high demand from exhibitors. France alone asked for and received some 80,000 square feet of wall space. Much of the statuary on display was earmarked for permanent display in and around Chicago at the close of the fair.

As the steamer continued south, passengers would view the Foreign Buildings, small structures surrounded by lawns, walks and beds of flowers

A First Impression

A sense of surprise, of delight, a suggestion of enchanted regions, come to one as he stands for the first time in the great court of the World's Fair.... The first [thought] is of the vast change which this object lesson will make in the minds of the millions who visit it, broadening, opening, lighting up dark corners, bringing them in sympathy with their fellow-men, sending them back to homes, however humble, with thoughts that will beautify and gladden entire lifetimes, furnishing a topic for countless winter nights' exchanges of opinions and themes of stories for generations yet unborn. It is safe to estimate that our civilization and advance in the liberal arts will be moved forward by a quarter of a century as the result of this marvellous Exposition.

The second thought is the ever present proof of the pleasure which this enchanted land brings to the millions who are visiting it....

It was my good fortune to be present on the Fourth of July, when the number of people on the grounds exceeded three hundred and five thousand. It was most interesting to study the faces, to note the looks of appreciation, to hear the exclamations of admiration, to listen to comment which was intelligent even when the garb was homely. I walked through many miles of avenues on that day: everywhere unmistakable signs of enjoyment, everywhere the comment of intelligent appreciation, and above all, everywhere the utmost good-nature. That, to my mind, was the most marvellous exhibition of all, that in a crowd containing more than three hundred thousand souls there was not, so far as I was able to see, and I carefully searched for it, one ill-tempered face, one drunken man. What a change has come over our civilization in the past twenty-five years!

Yet here were only happy, smiling faces, women and children moving with perfect freedom, without even a thought that they were in the largest crowd of people ever brought together within a single enclosure upon the American continent, all feeling kindly toward each other, all taking part in the general joy and universal pride that this was the creation of their countrymen. The contrasts between the stage-coach and giant locomotive, between the birch-bark letter of the Indian and the telautograph message of Gray, the canoe of the Esquimaux and the electric railway, were not so great as that between the customs prevalent in my boyhood and this realization of hopes for a new civilization in the midst of which I walked on this Fourth of July, 1893.

—John Brisben Walker, *The World's Fair Numbers of The Cosmopolitan* [Magazine], 1893

One of the most striking views of the fairgrounds was from the obelisk at the south end of the South Canal. From here, a vista nearly one mile long unfolded in glistening waters and graceful bridges, stately statues and gleaming buildings.

and shrubbery, ornamented with statuary. On the lakefront were the buildings erected by France, Ceylon, Norway, Germany, Spain, Canada and Great Britain. Some twelve additional Foreign Buildings were located just west. Like the State Buildings, the foreign structures varied in architectural design and color, reflecting characteristics of their homeland. Many other foreign nations elected not to erect costly headquarters buildings, but to sponsor exhibits in the Great Buildings or on the Midway.

Piers, Fisheries, Woman's Building and Midway

Coming abreast of the southeastern tip of the Foreign Buildings area, the steamer would clear the North and Naval piers, reaching like great arms into Lake Michigan. There passengers would see the replica of the battleship *Illinois*, a massive vessel fitted with guns, turrets, torpedo tubes, nets and booms, boats, anchors and chains. The "ship" would appear to be moored to the Naval Pier, but in fact was sitting on piling.

Wooded Island was intended to provide a quiet resting spot for satiated sightseers. Here, they could relax on benches, stroll the walkways and visit the Japanese Ho-o-den. At night, the "fairy lamps" (little glass cups of various colors covering tiny lights of wick and oil) transformed the island into a magical fairyland.

*The site allotted to the Fisheries Building was so irregular that it required a particularly remarkable structure. Architect Henry Ives Cobb answered the challenge with a collection of three graceful pavilions connected by curved arcades. **Inset**: The arcade of the Fisheries Building was decorated with intricate depictions of marine life, such as frogs, tortoises, serpents and reeds.*

Just south of the Foreign Buildings, directly inland from the Naval Pier, was a considerable expanse of the Main Lagoon, with an inlet to the lake. In the center of the lagoon, though out of view from the steamer, was the Wooded Island, one of the most charming spots in the exposition. Actually part of the horticultural exhibit, the sixteen-acre island featured lavish gardens and graceful walks following a serpentine course. On the north end of the island was a collection of lovely Japanese buildings called the Ho-o-den. Just to the south, on a tiny island, was Hunter's Cabin, featuring Davy Crockett relics.

To the east of the main lagoon on a banana-shaped island was the Fisheries Building, one of the smallest of the Great Buildings, but a showpiece nevertheless. Designed by Henry Ives Cobb of Chicago, it included a 162-foot by 362-foot main building flanked by a curved arcade and polygonal pavilion on each end. The building was Romanesque in design, with a Spanish tile roof. An interesting feature of the exterior was an ingenious arrangement of capitals, brackets, cornices and other ornamental details which were decorated with thousands of fish and other representations of sea life. Inside was said to be the most spectacular collection of marine plants and critters ever displayed. Ten huge aquariums and many smaller ones with a total capacity of 140,000 gallons of water and 3,000 square feet of surface

This view from atop the U.S. Government Building shows the bridge approach to Wooded Island and the Japanese Ho-o-den from the west pavilion of the Fisheries Building. Directly behind the island is the Woman's Building. Across the avenue to the right of the Woman's Building is the Bureau of Public Comfort and next to it, the domed Illinois Building.

This photograph, taken from the top of the Ferris Wheel, shows the eastern end of the Midway Plaisance and the many domes of the White City beyond.

featured virtually every form of sea life known to man. Although elaborate aquariums are fairly common today, the fisheries exhibit at the Chicago Fair was considered unique by nineteenth-century standards. A total of 80,000 gallons of water were circulated in the saltwater displays. The saltwater was obtained from the Atlantic Ocean, evaporated to reduce both its quantity and weight for transportation, and then, once at the fairgrounds, restored to its proper density with freshwater from Lake Michigan.

On the west side of the main lagoon was the Woman's Building, a graceful Italian Renaissance structure designed by a recent MIT graduate, Sophia Hayden of Boston. Luxuriant shrubs and beds of fragrant flowers encircled the building. Directly in front, the lagoon took the form of a bay. A staircase led from a landing at the center to a terrace six feet high and the main triple-arched entrance. The building featured a central pavilion flanked by corner pavilions connected at the first story by open arcades. The arcades formed a

A Triumph for Women

When officials authorized a building at the World's Columbian Exposition devoted exclusively to women they thought they were simply following protocol set by other world's fairs and perhaps placating a few women's groups vying for display space. Little did they know that they would create the framework for a force that would advance women's rights and recognition far into the next century.

In addition to allocating space for women's exhibits, the fair's framers determined that the building would be designed, decorated and managed entirely by women—giving them unprecedented control in a world-scale event. A 117-member Board of Lady Managers, composed of representatives from every state and territory, was formed to manage the building. They did so with gusto.

Bertha Honore Palmer, a Chicago socialite and wife of business tycoon Potter Palmer, was elected as president of the board. Described as a "social leader with a social conscience," Palmer proved her mettle in short time. Extremely resourceful, energetic and skilled in executive ability, she inspired women of all nations with her enthusiasm and planned a systematic campaign to show the male-dominated world that "ability is not a matter of sex."

One of the board's first steps was to find a female architect for the project. Because there were very few women architects in the 1890s, the board launched a nationwide competition among student and professional women architects. The winning submission came from 21-year-old Sophia Hayden, a recent graduate of MIT who designed a "delicate and graceful" Italian Renaissance villa.

In seeking the best of women's achievements, the Lady Managers sent formal invitations to every country in the world to submit displays, met with female sovereigns to obtain help in promoting the event and organized boards in every state in the nation to solicit works from American women.

The response was overwhelming. Submissions flooded in from every corner of the world. The Woman's Building overflowed with displays of women's achievements in every imaginable branch of

Above the main, triple-arched entrance to the Woman's Building was an open balcony and a pediment decorated with bas-relief representations of women's occupations such as "Beneficence," "Literature," "Art" and "Home Life."

industry, science and art from prehistoric eras to the present. The displays were not of ordinary works, but were those judged (by a female jury) to be the best in their field. Paintings, engravings, sculpture, needlework and ceramics by women filled the grand skylit gallery. Women's accomplishments in science, health care, philanthropy, literature, invention, architecture, education and exploration crammed every inch of the pavilion. From daybreak to dusk women leaders of the decade took to the stage to present their research and views on everything from financial planning and preventive medicine to educational needs and nonsexist child-rearing. (Interestingly, there was only one presentation on women's health issues, according to *World's Fair*: "A woman doctor clad in bloomers told an audience of whalebone-encased ladies that tight lacing was responsible for more than fifty female health disorders.")

Women's organizations also were prominent in the building. In fact, so many women's groups clamored for separate quarters that they threatened to overrun the entire building. The board finally ripped out walls and crammed some sixty organizations, ranging from the huge Woman's Christian Temperance Union to Susan B. Anthony and her company of suffragettes, into one hall.

There were no competitive exhibits in the Woman's Building as there were in the other Great Buildings. Many women's works were entered in competitions conducted in the appropriate Great Buildings where they could compete with those by male entrants. The Lady Managers insisted on this strategy, according to one report: "Restricting women exhibitors to one building would have been a fatal blow, for awards received in competition only with the work of other women would have been of comparatively little actual commercial value."

Although some of the contemporary works displayed by women were lambasted by critics (including then-unknown Mary Cassatt's avant-garde mural *Modern Woman*), most fairgoers were surprised and impressed by the overall display.

The World's Columbian Exposition helped advance the cause of women's suffrage and launch careers for women in fields previously considered taboo. But more than anything else, the fair helped position women as a force to be reckoned with in *all* arenas as the world crossed into the twentieth century.

The eastern veranda of the Woman's Building was decorated with beautiful vases of hanging flowers contributed by French gardeners. Here, after they "paid a dollar each for Isabella quarter dollars, looked at Marie Bashkirtseff's last picture; drank Ceylon tea, inquired for Mrs. Potter Palmer, got dinner on the roof-garden or, better yet, heard some famous woman lecture on the needed reforms of the age," visitors could sit and gaze across the lagoon at the U.S. Government Building or northward upon the expansive Illinois Building.

shady promenade the entire 388-foot length of the building. Beautiful hanging gardens adorned the structure. Immediately inside the front entrance were a model hospital on the left and a model kindergarten on the right.

Perhaps the most significant thing about the Woman's Building was the simple fact of its existence. While one could easily argue the arcane nature of a building devoted to "the importance of women," the role of women at the fair was a breakthrough a century ago. The building was designed, decorated

The Great Buildings

Administration Building

Architect: Richard M. Hunt, New York

Size: Four pavilions 84 ft x 84 ft connected by an octagonal, drum-supporting, ribbed dome

Cost: $650,000

Agricultural Building

Architect: McKim, Mead & White, New York

Size: 800 ft x 500 ft; annex 550 ft x 300 ft

Cost: $618,000

Anthropology Building

Architect: Charles B. Atwood, Chicago

Size: 415 ft x 225 ft

Cost: $88,000

Electricity Building

Architect: Van Brunt & Howe, Kansas City

Size: 690 ft x 345 ft

Cost: $410,000

Fisheries Building

Architect: Henry Ives Cobb, Chicago

Size: 162 ft x 362 ft; two annexes 135 ft in diameter

Cost: $225,000

Forestry Building

Architect: Charles B. Atwood, Chicago

Size: 208 ft x 528 ft

Cost: $100,000

Horticultural Building

Architect: Jenney & Mundie, Chicago

Size: 998 ft x 250 ft; eight greenhouses 24 ft x 100 ft

Cost: $300,000

Machinery Hall

Architect: Peabody & Stearns, Boston

Size: 842 ft x 492 ft; annex 490 ft x 550 ft

Cost: $1.2 million

Manufactures and Liberal Arts Building

Architect: George B. Post, New York

Size: 1,687 ft x 787 ft

Cost: $1.7 million

Mines and Mining Building

Architect: S. S. Beman, Chicago

Size: 700 ft x 350 ft

Cost: $265,000

Palace of Fine Arts

Architect: Charles B. Atwood, Chicago

Size: 320 ft x 500 ft; two annexes 120 ft x 200 ft

Cost: $670,000

Transportation Building

Architect: Adler and Sullivan, Chicago

Size: 256 ft x 960 ft; annex 425 ft x 900 ft

Cost: $370,000

U.S. Government Building

Architect: Willoughby J. Edbrooke, Washington, D.C.

Size: 420 ft x 350 ft

Cost: $325,000

Woman's Building

Architect: Sophia G. Hayden, Boston

Size: 199 ft x 388 ft

Cost: $138,000

The upper promenade of the Administration Building supported huge gas torches that were lit at night to illuminate the building's enormous golden dome. At right is one of the eight groups of angels trumpeting the victory of peace. In one of the many mishaps during construction of the exposition, one of these angelic groups broke loose as it was being lifted into place on the promenade, landing with one wing stuck in the frozen ground and the rest of it shattered. Note the Ferris Wheel at left.

and, most important, managed by women. Every country in the world had contributed examples of their finest achievements by women in all endeavors imaginable. The central gallery showcased women's best in art, authorship and handicraft. Other galleries displayed charitable and industrial work. Interestingly, there were no competitive art exhibits in this building, only displays.

Looking west, beyond the Woman's Building, were the delights of the Midway Plaisance, the one-mile stretch of land featuring myriad displays and amusements offered by private vendors, many of them from foreign countries. The Midway was not considered part of the exposition proper, but drew some of the largest crowds. One of the highlights was the famous Ferris Wheel which passengers could ride for fifty cents—a price equal to the admission fee for the fair itself.

Horticultural, Government, Manufactures and Liberal Arts

Just south of the entrance to the Midway, opposite the Wooded Island, was the Horticultural Building. Surrounded by elaborate gardens, this "Venetian Renaissance" structure designed by Jenney & Mundie, featured a glass dome and roof to provide light for the world's most extensive collection of

This view of the nearly completed Horticultural Building shows the beauty of its huge glass domes and friezes decorated with chubby cherubs and vines. By the time the fair opened, the grounds around the building were filled with magnificent displays of pansies, lush gardens and huge vases of flowers.

horticultural products. The building was nearly 1,000 feet long with a main pavilion and two end pavilions connected in such a way as to create beautiful interior courts. The building featured terraces inside and out, and obviously, the floral landscaping was the most elaborate on the grounds. One of the most ambitious displays here was from California. The Southern California Fair Association took nearly 24,000 square feet in this building alone, and outside, the California Growers Association showed a five-acre orchard in full bloom.

In or near the building (including plantings on Wooded Island), there were five acres for a nursery, 19,200 square feet of greenhouse space, a half million pansies, 100,000 roses and millions of other flowers.

Flanking the Horticultural Building on the south was the Choral Hall, a Doric-order structure resembling an amphitheater. This hall was one of several auxiliary buildings erected by the exposition sponsors. On either side of the flight of steps leading up to the main entrance were statues of Handel and

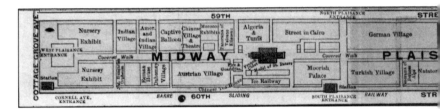

While not its most glamorous profile, the south side of the Manufactures and Liberal Arts Building was probably the most familiar to fairgoers. This was the side facing the Court of Honor, seen from the northeast corner of Machinery Hall, with one of the electric fountains in the immediate foreground and the MacMonnies or Columbian Fountain to the left. The Manufactures and Liberal Arts Building was the giant of the fair, covering more than thirty acres. It was said that a fairgoer could spend ten hours a day for a month inside the cavernous structure and still not see it all.

THE WORLD'S COLUMBIAN EXPOSITION

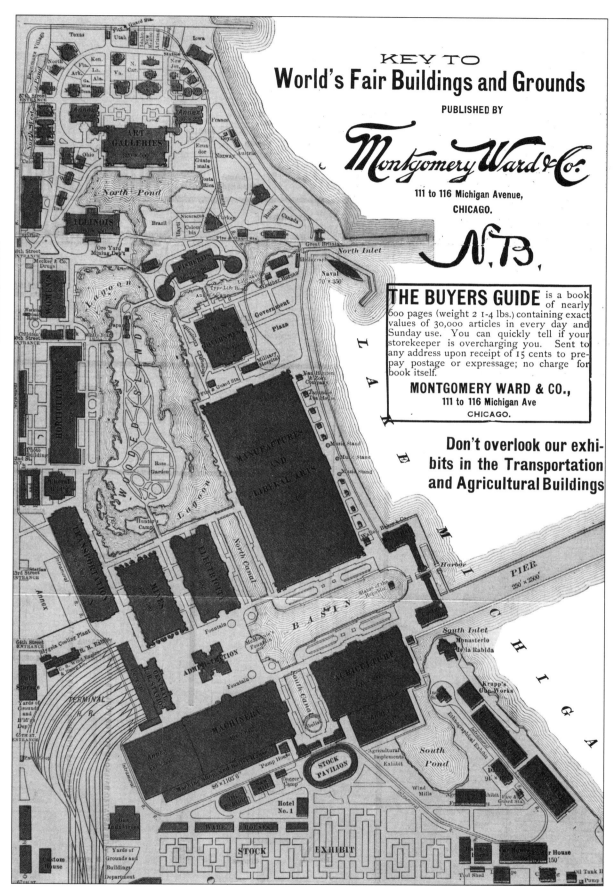

Looking southeast from the Illinois Building, this view shows the serene byways that led to Wooded Island with its Japanese Ho-o-den at right, the Fisheries Building on the left, the mammoth Manufactures and Liberal Arts Building at center and the Electricity and Mines and Mining buildings in the background, at right.

THE WORLD'S COLUMBIAN EXPOSITION

Several chocolate concessionaires erected buildings to tempt passersby with delicious confections.

Bach. Panels above the door were adorned with relief portraits of Gluck, Berlioz, Wagner, Schumann, Schubert, Mozart, Mendelssohn, Bach, Handel and Beethoven. This music lover's paradise was equally grand on the inside, with its stately columns and 2,500-person choir.

As the steamer passed the piers, the U.S. Government Building would come into view, a gleaming structure of iron and glass with an imposing central dome. The building was classical in style. In addition to exhibits from the U.S. Post Office, War, Treasury, Fisheries, Agriculture and Interior departments, there were many exquisite treasures from the Smithsonian Institution. Among the most fascinating were an exhibit of every piece of paper money ever issued by the U.S. government, the first typewriter and the famous "Long Tom" gun which served America so well in the War of 1812. On the lakeshore east of the building the government displayed a gun battery, a lifesaving station, lighthouse, war balloons and the battleship *Illinois*.

But passengers' eyes would rest here only momentarily, for next door sat the massive Manufactures and Liberal Arts Building, by far the largest and most physically imposing building of the exposition. Nearly 1,700 feet by 800 feet, this giant, Corinthian-ornamented edifice stretched one-third of a mile along the lakefront and covered more than thirty acres. The mammoth size and visual strength of this building made it almost overpowering, as it seemed to stretch out and then fade into the distance, never quite ending.

Inside, building architects and fair designers had attempted to create a floor plan that would allow fairgoers to appreciate the wealth of displays without being overwhelmed by the sheer volume.

An interior view of the U.S. Government Building

The Electricity Building, with its 170-foot-high spires surmounting pavilions at each corner of the structure, presented a charming view whether from the waters of the lagoon or the Wooded Island.

The building was so huge that it even had a fifty-foot-wide avenue inside. "Columbia Avenue" channeled people the length of the main floor. A gallery fifty feet wide extended around the entire building, adding another eight acres of floor space. Projecting from the main gallery were eighty-six smaller galleries, twelve feet wide, from which visitors could survey the vast array of exhibits and the busy scene below. Thirty staircases led to the galleries. The building's massive roof, with nearly a 400-foot free span, was constructed of iron and glass. The trusses were reported to contain as much metal as the Brooklyn Bridge! In fact, the building required twelve million pounds of steel in its trusses, two million pounds of iron and three million feet of lumber. Designed by George B. Post of New York, the building's exterior was finished in staff, treated to look like marble. Great fluted pilasters and immense archways, also made of staff, encircled the building.

The Manufactures and Liberal Arts Building was truly a "world's fair" in its own right, documenting and displaying the progress of mankind in every section of the globe. Visitors could easily spend a month in this building alone inspecting the products of the world's achievements in science, art, industry and intellectual development and refinement.

Electricity, Mines, Transportation

In the shadow of the Manufactures and Liberal Arts Building to the west, blocked from the steamer's view, were the Electricity and Mines and Mining buildings. Both structures were of "Renaissance" design and covered a little more than five acres each. The Electricity Building, a spacious and stately rectangular structure, featured such architectural delights as a continuous

The imposing facade illustrates the massive and yet graceful proportions of the Mines and Mining Building. The grand central arch, 140 feet high, and domed pavilions were supported by heavy pilasters composed of granite blocks. The lofty bays, recessed balcony with pillared support, elaborate frieze, architectural reliefs and bannered flagstaffs add the finishing touches of beauty.

Corinthian order of pilasters forty-two feet high on the exterior and a pavilion at each corner of the building topped by open spires or towers rising 170 feet into the air. Some 40,000 panes of glass were used in the building—more than in any other single structure at the fair. An open portico ran along the entire southern facade. The building's pavilions were furnished with elaborate windows and balconies. The exterior was decorated with rich details and friezes, pediments, panels and spandrels, all with architectural motifs representative of the building's theme. At night the building was illuminated with thousands of tiny lights to create one of the most spectacular evening attractions of the fair.

Greeting fairgoers at the main entrance to the Electricity Building was a fifteen-foot-high statue of Benjamin Franklin, dressed in colonial garb and holding the implements of his famous discovery: a key, silk kite-cord and umbrella. Thomas Edison, the foremost electrical inventor of the time, was a key contributor to the success of the Electricity Building. His company reportedly invested half a million dollars in displays.

Next door was one of the simplest buildings in design, the Mining Building or "Hall of Mines and Mining." Approximately 700 feet by 350 feet, it sported enormous arched facades, richly embellished with sculptural decoration emblematic of mining and allied industries. Over the main doorway was a colossal, half-reclining female figure in Greek drapery, holding a miner's lamp in one hand and a pick in the other. More than one and a half million pounds of steel and iron were used in the construction of this building.

Main portal of the Mines and Mining Building

Benjamin Franklin *at the entrance to Electricity Building*

Northwest of the Mines and Mining Building was the fanciful Transportation Building, designed by Adler and Sullivan. In design this structure was a major departure from the classical style of the other Great Buildings. It was also the only Great Building not finished in white alone, featuring magnificent shades of red. Although it was Romanesque in general style, it had a rather Islamic look. It was exquisitely refined and simple, with clean lines and a low-pitched roof. Its interior was treated much like a basilica with a broad nave and side aisles. The roof was in three sections, the central one rising high above the others to form a 165-foot-high cupola. Visitors could ride one of eight elevators to reach the observation deck for a grand view of the grounds, lake and surrounding country. The building's main entrance was an immense single arch known as the "Golden Doorway." Although not actually gold, the doorway was stunning in its intricate green and silver etched metal design, and was enriched with extraordinary carvings, bas-reliefs and murals featuring transportation themes.

In many regards, the Transportation Building was one of the most im-

portant of the fair. This was the first time that a world's fair had devoted such time, energy and space to the subject. Inside, every mode and device of transportation known, from baby carriages to locomotives, was displayed.

Directly to the west, the Transportation Annexes occupied a nine-acre triangular parcel of land. These buildings were, in effect, railroad museums filled with full-size, sixteen-foot track sections and more than 100 locomotives, as well as other passenger and freight cars.

Directly south was the main railroad terminal, where two dozen different lines shuttled people to the fairgrounds from all parts of Chicago and beyond.

Casino, Pier, Peristyle, Court of Honor

While passengers were still staring in awe at the buildings onshore, the steamer would come to rest at its destination, the Casino Pier. Hardy visitors could then walk the 2,500-foot length of the pier to the main gates. But most of the 100,000 people per day who arrived by steamer chose to pay ten cents

While all of the Great Buildings differed somewhat in architectural style, the Transportation Building represented the boldest departure from classical design and coloration. Much of the exterior was painted in red and decorated with multi-colored foliate motifs. The angels adorning the facade were cut in linen and glued to the exterior.

Inset: *The "Golden Doorway" on the east side of the Transportation Building was the most ornate of all building entrances at the fair. This grand portal featured a series of receding arches entirely overlaid in gold leaf, which actually projected a silvery-green color. The space immediately above the entry was ornamented with striking allegorical figures and groups in bas-relief. On one side appeared in panel "an original study in ancient transportation," and on the opposite side, "the palatial accessories of modern railway travel."*

Above: The Peristyle, with its forty-eight columns representing every state and territory in the nation, connected the Music Hall (at left) and the Casino (barely in view at the right). Visitors who arrived at the Casino Pier and rode the Movable Sidewalk to shore entered the fairgrounds through the triumphal arch at the center of the Peristyle.

Left: This humbling view from within the Peristyle shows the immense size of the pillars supporting the grand entrance to the fair. The huge Corinthian columns were made of lath and plaster but supported the weight of a double row of immense statues. Sadly, the glorious structure burned to the ground in a fire in January 1894.

Most of the 100,000 people who arrived by steamer each day splurged on the Movable Sidewalk with its ten-cent fare to ride the length of the pier to the entrance of the exposition.

Columbian Arch at the center of the Peristyle

and board the wondrous Movable Sidewalk with its comfortable chairs that would carry them to shore.

When they stepped off the sidewalk they would embrace an enchanting view of the fairgrounds. Even their preview from the lake had not prepared first-time visitors for the enormity and grandeur before them.

Directly ahead was the magnificent Peristyle, a series of columns connecting the Music Hall to the north and the Casino, on the south. Each of the forty-eight columns of the Peristyle bore a state or territory's name, coat-of-arms and an emblematic statue. At the center of the structure was a grand archway, dedicated to Columbus and inscribed with the names of the world's great explorers. Looking through the archway from Lake Michigan, visitors would see the glorious Court of Honor, the central area of the fair encompassing the Grand Basin and a dramatic grouping of the Great Buildings. Emerging from the waters of the basin was the *Statue of the Republic*, an immense figure representing liberty with an eagle resting on a globe in one hand and a staff supporting a liberty cap in the other. The statue's beauty "would satisfy the sculpture of the old Greek school," according to one guidebook.

Many other statues and fountains graced the shimmering waters and the expansive avenues surrounding them. Opposite the *Statue of the Republic*, at the head of the Grand Basin, was perhaps the most imposing group of statuary on the grounds: *MacMonnies Fountain*. This fountain depicted a triumphal barge, carrying a victorious *Columbia*, with *Fame* at the prow. The barge was propelled by oars in the hands of eight female figures personifying the arts, sciences and industry and guided by the hand of *Time*. Eight outriders on sea horses cleared the way through the splashing foam. The

Sculptor Frederick MacMonnies created MacMonnies or Columbian Fountain, *said to be the largest fountain in the world in 1893, at a cost of $48,000. The thirty-seven figures incorporated in the fountain stood in the center of a circular pool at the western end of the Grand Basin. The central element, a barge symbolizing the* Ship of State, *was heralded by* Fame *at the prow and guided by* Father Time *at the helm, and was propelled by eight maidens representing industry and the arts. The crowning glory was* Columbia *enthroned on a central pedestal. Sea horses with riders, dolphins, mermaids and tritons sprung from the water surrounding the barge. Although criticized by some for being a bit overdone,* MacMonnies Fountain *was a big crowd-pleaser, especially at night when colored searchlights played upon the scene.*

Above: The Court of Honor represented the formal expression of Frederick Law Olmsted's elaborate master plan. It featured the most dramatic grouping of Great Buildings and the Grand Basin.

Left: Ancient civilizations delighted in heroic statues, such as the Colossus of Rhodes, the Egyptian Sphinx, Jupiter and Olympia, but World's Columbian Exposition planners chose a more modern model for their Grand Basin. The Statue of the Republic, the ultimate symbol of liberty, rose sixty-five feet from a platform at the east end of the basin. The statue had been built in the Forestry Building following a sixteen-foot-high working model. The total cost was $25,000, including $8,000 for the sculptor and $1,400 in gold leaf finish.

In Industry, a huge statue appearing on the Administration Building, a mother at her spinning wheel is "tempted by love to leave her work for a moment."

The Columbian Fire Department tests its monstrous hoses in a display in the Grand Basin on the northern side of the Agricultural Building. Saint-Gaudens' famous Diana *is poised on the central dome.*

Below: The Columbian Exposition's emergency crew poses aboard the F. D. Millet, *named for the fair's director of decoration. Skilled climbers and swimmers, these men were trained to "climb to the highest point on the grounds or to jump into the lagoon," which they patrolled at night. They were called on numerous times, particularly during evening parades, swimming contests and fireworks.*

fountain spewed streams of water from some 100 jets—a magnificent sight by day or night.

Agricultural, Machinery, Administration

On the south side of the Grand Basin, near the shore of Lake Michigan, was the Agricultural Building, described as "bold and heroic." Designed by McKim, Mead & White in a "Roman" style, it encompassed a half-million square feet and featured several ornate domes, including a central one 130 feet in diameter. On top of this dome was sculptor Augustus Saint-Gaudens' beautiful *Statue of Diana.* The statue had originally been designed for Madison Square Garden in New York, but proved to be too large. Pronounced a "masterpiece of American art," it also acted as a weather vane, shifting with the slightest change in the wind.

Connected to the Agricultural Building by a colonnade rounding the South Canal of the Grand Basin was Machinery Hall. This "Palace of Mechanic Arts" was nearly identical to the Agricultural Building in size and cost, but differed markedly in appearance. Classical in design, with Spanish Renaissance detail, it was considered one of the most magnificent buildings in pure beauty. It was spanned by three arched 125-foot trusses which made the interior look like three large train houses side by side.

The iron trusses were built separately so that they could be sold as railway train houses after the fair. In each of the long naves inside the building there was an elevated traveling crane, running the length of the 842-foot building, used to move machinery. Power for this building was supplied by a huge powerplant on the south side of the building.

North of Machinery Hall was the impressive Administration Building. Occupying one of the most commanding positions on the grounds, reportedly to acknowledge its world-renowned architect Richard M. Hunt, this building was generally regarded as a major focal point of the fair due to its towering dome, prominent location and imposing design. Although it was "only" 260 feet by 260 feet, it was particularly conspicuous because of its location in an open court at the head of the Grand Basin and because of its huge gilded

The Administration Building held a sovereign position among all the wonders of the fair. Besides serving as a headquarters for fair officials, its spacious rotunda offered a favorite meeting-place for fairgoers. Four square pavilions surrounded a beautiful French octagonal gilded dome which bore stunning ornamentation in relief.

By night, the Administration Building and the Grand Basin were a sight to behold. Thousands of tiny lights illuminated the grounds, waterways, walkways and buildings in the Court of Honor. The Administration Building was particularly spectacular, glittering like a spaceship against the black sky. As part of the light show huge searchlights directed their beams on various fountains and statues, in alternating colors of white, green, blue, purple, yellow and scarlet.

dome. The dome, literally and figuratively the high point of the Court of Honor, was 120 feet in diameter and 220 feet high. In addition to the dome, the building comprised four 84-foot-square pavilions. The large plot of ground surrounding the building was the site of bandstands, presentations by dignitaries and other major events. Inside the building were the headquarters of the numerous officials connected with the management and administration of the exposition.

Forestry, Anthropology, Stock Pavilion

Southeast of the Agricultural Building, on the shores of Lake Michigan, were the Forestry and Anthropology buildings. The former, patterned after the Forestry Building at the 1889 Paris Exposition (only three times larger),

Above: The east side of Machinery Hall faced the South Canal. This Spanish Renaissance-ornamented structure featured large central towers with bells that chimed every night at six, and smaller cupolas at the corners.

Left: The grand loggia or veranda of Machinery Hall overlooking the parade ground in front of the Terminal Station was an exhibit in itself. It was rich in detail, with grilled windows, paneled ceiling, ornate door-casings, brilliantly colored murals, Corinthian columns, fluted pilasters and a beautiful balustrade.

Although low and unpretentious in appearance, the Forestry Building was perhaps the only building at the World's Columbian Exposition that would not seem out of place at a twentieth-century fair. It was built almost entirely of wood, with tree trunks donated by several states used as columns.

had a somewhat rustic design. Not surprisingly, the main material used in its construction was wood. A veranda with a colonnade of tree trunks supporting a thatched roof surrounded the building. A wide variety of trees, from the delicately smooth and silvery birch to the roughest and reddest-barked pines, had been contributed by different states and foreign countries. The building's lower walls were made of shingles and its clerestory walls were made of a variety of woods arranged in geometric patterns. Windows were trimmed with small debarked half logs. The main entrance was finished in different woods carved by craftsmen throughout the world. The interior was also made entirely of wood.

Built to accommodate the overflow exhibits of the liberal arts section of the Manufactures and Liberal Arts Building, the Anthropology Building (officially part of the exposition's Ethnological Department) encompassed many exhibits outside the boundaries of its 415-foot by 225-foot structure. The painstaking reproductions of the *Nina, Pinta* and *Santa Maria* were located in the South Pond directly in front of the building. The reproduction of a 1,000-year-old Viking ship from Norway was moored to the north near the Naval Pier in Lake Michigan. Other compelling exhibits were the Indian Villages, the Yucatan Ruins and the Cliff Dwellers. After the fair, many exhibits from this

A thrilling elevator ride to the observation deck of the Manufactures and Liberal Arts Building gave sightseers a sweeping view over the Grand Basin to the southern end of the fairgrounds.

Fairgoers reportedly were slow to take advantage of the fifty motor launches and gondolas that transported passengers to many of the Great Buildings or simply on a relaxing tour of the maze of waterways. Described as "fine specimens of naval architecture," each of the thirty-five-foot boats carried thirty passengers on a circuitous route around the fairgrounds. This photo most likely was taken on one of the early days of the fair or early in the morning before the gates opened when there were virtually no lines for the motor launch. This boarding area in the lagoon west of the Manufactures and Liberal Arts Building advertised that its launches departed at "minute intervals."

Inset: This illustration from The Columbian Gallery shows several of the sixty Venetian gondolas that carried passengers through the waterways of the exposition. The craft were propelled by European gondoliers dressed in the red jackets and red and white striped breeches customary four centuries earlier. The gondolas were equipped with musicians playing guitars and mandolins.

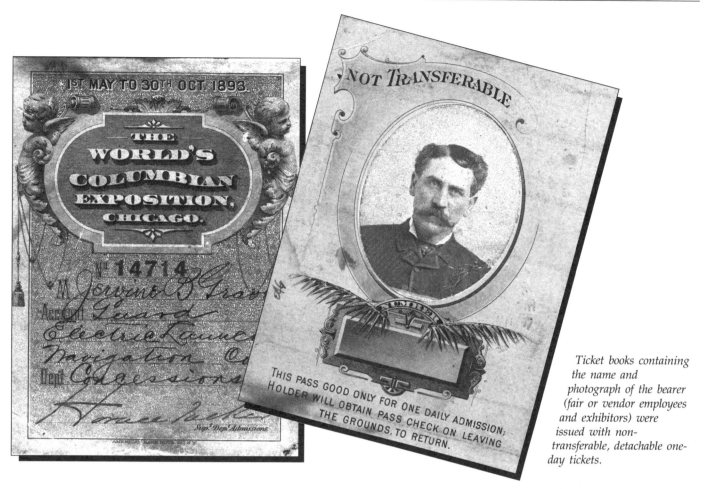

Ticket books containing the name and photograph of the bearer (fair or vendor employees and exhibitors) were issued with non-transferable, detachable one-day tickets.

department were transferred to permanent displays in the Palace of Fine Arts which became Chicago's Field Museum of Natural History—today the Chicago Museum of Science and Industry.

Between the Anthropology Building and the Casino Pier was the Monastery of La Rabida, a facsimile of the quaint structure in which Columbus found refuge and finalized his plans to sail across the Atlantic in search of the New World. Some of the most valuable exhibits of the fair were housed in the monastery, including rare Columbiana, the first map of the world, Queen Isabella's will and relics of the first Christian church.

Perhaps the only area lacking ornate facades, heroic statuary or world-class artwork was the forty-acre portion of the southern fairgrounds reserved for livestock displays. Although by its nature this area was not elaborate in architectural accomplishment, it did feature a large show ring and myriad displays of livestock from around the world.

In addition to the Great Buildings and Auxiliary, State and Foreign buildings, numerous private or corporate buildings dotted the grounds at every turn. Among them were the Krupp Gun Exhibit, the Puck Building, the White Star Building and the New England Clam Bake. Other private exhibitors purchased display space within major exhibit halls.

Stunning architecture, from that of the smallest pavilion to the grandest hall, was certainly the most awe-inspiring feature of the exposition; but inside the buildings many wonders of the world awaited.

Kaleife and his "ship of the desert" were key attractions at the "Wild East Show" on the Midway.

III

The Exhibits and Attractions

OFFICIALS PEGGED THE NUMBER OF EXHIBITS at the World's Columbian Exposition at around 65,000, with the number of individual items totaling in the millions. The numbers were mind-boggling. The official guidebooks, programs and reference books of the day couldn't cover all of the displays, or even agree on the most outstanding. One hundred years later it is simply impossible to mention every exhibit. The following pages highlight the displays in all of the major buildings, on the grounds and along the Midway. Though representing only a smattering of the exhibits, these highlights hopefully will give readers a sense of the many and varied wonders of the fair.

The Great Buildings

The Great Buildings housed the most valuable, most extensive and most striking displays presented by exhibitors. The only Great Building that did not offer exhibits was the Administration Building, which served strictly as a headquarters for fair managers.

Agricultural Building

Grains, grains and more grains of every size, type and configuration seemed to dominate this building. Some were presented in intricate murals, others in towering pyramids. There were breads and biscuits, starches and pastes, sugars and syrups, malts and liquors. All types of meat and dairy products, every fruit and vegetable known to man in both seed and flowering state was there. Also shown were the animals, machines, tools and processes used to produce the goods, the pests and pesticides common to farming, plus model farm buildings, farm management classes, weather stations and

Above: One of the six general admission tickets to the exposition was designed to illustrate the era in American history when Indians ruled the land.

experimental colleges. There were cocoa mills, chocolate pavilions, breweries and a moonshiner's cabin. There were more than one hundred exhibits of tobacco and an equal number devoted to nuts. The list goes on and on, but the following are a few of the eye-catchers.

Cork: Cork trees, rough bark in bales and manufactured cork, such as that used in hats and insoles, created an interesting exhibit.

Egyptian Cigarette Booth: A cigarette manufacturer from Cairo displayed his wares in a beautiful booth fashioned after an Egyptian temple, adorned with a sphinx and pyramids.

Farm Products: Every state and territory in the Union submitted farm products for this building. Each was labeled with the producer's name, where the product was grown, character of the soil, date of planting, quantity of seed used, weather conditions, method of cultivation, irrigation system used, date of harvesting, yield per acre, weight and price of product at nearest market. Many European and Central American countries placed displays here as well.

Liberty Bell Reproduction: Pennsylvania's exhibit included a "Liberty Bell" made of wheat, oats and rye, complete with a crack which was covered with wisps of straw.

Don Quixote would never have charged the army of windmills displayed at the World's Columbian Exposition. This huge collection, blazing in all colors and whirling at tremendous speed, created a fascinating display beside the pond outside the Agricultural Building. Every type and size of the labor-saving contrivance could be seen, from the old Dutch windmill made famous in poetry to the latest patented American invention. Many manufacturers participated, with wooden versions, as well as steel and iron.

THE WORLD'S COLUMBIAN EXPOSITION

Above: Crowds gather for a chance to sample the free fruit that California would hand out on September 9, 1893.
Below: This immense picture of the ideal Illinois prairie farm was created entirely of grains and grasses. The frame was made of yellow corn-ears. The farmhouse, barns and stock sheds in the picture were made with corn husks and seeds. The mosaic hung in the Illinois Building.

San Diego fruit growers fashioned this "Liberty Bell," crack and all, with oranges, lemons and grapefruit. Nearby, other California cities displayed arrangements of grapes, raisins, olives and olive oil.

Left: To create these American Standards of Humanity, *a Harvard professor measured the anatomical features of some 25,000 American subjects. The statues were displayed in the Anthropology Building.* ***Below:*** *"Medicine" and "Plenty Horse" were two of the Sioux Indian chiefs that could be seen along with representatives from a number of other American Indian tribes in Indian Village.*

Monster Cheese: A 22,000-pound mass of cheese, encased in iron, was presented by Canada. It was the work of more than 1,600 maids who had milked 10,000 cows to produce the 27,000 gallons of milk used in the cheese.

Ostriches: Cape Colony went all out with displays of the world's most powerful bird. Bright plumes decorated the doorways to the exhibit, polished ostrich eggs hung from the windows, and a pyramid of daintily colored eggs rose from the center of the room.

Pickle Map: Not to be outdone by the Liberty Bell, a Pennsylvania firm displayed an 18- by 24-foot map of the United States made entirely of pickles, vinegar and spices.

Schlitz Brewery: This pavilion's interior was in the shape of two immense beer casks.

Women's Silk Culture: A big draw to female visitors, this display demonstrated the silk-making process, showing silk worms feeding on mulberry leaves, jars full of cocoons, raw silk, dyed silk and finished silk fabrics.

Anthropology Building

This hall was a storehouse of physical science tracing the development of the human race from prehistoric times to the present. It featured the relics

This great Siberian mammoth was a reproduction of "the largest animal that has developed among the quadrupeds of the earth." To create the display, a professor took measurements from the bones of a mammoth housed in the Royal Museum in Stuttgart, Germany. He then visited the Russian Imperial Museum in St. Petersburg to study the remains of another mammoth that had been found in 1799 in a glacier in northern Siberia, its flesh and hair preserved by cold temperatures.

of aborigines, cave dwellers, lake dwellers and cliff dwellers; the model homes of prehistoric man; glimpses into the domestic life of the ancient Romans unearthed from the ashes of Pompeii; and the stories of Egyptian pharaohs. Highlights of some of the most notable exhibits follow.

Adam and Eve: A Harvard professor took measurements of some sixty anatomical features from 25,000 American subjects to create these "typical" forms of American manhood and womanhood.

Bolivian Indians: Among the eighteen Indians in this display was one of the largest men in the world—a 25-year-old man who was purported to be nine feet ten inches tall (a height never attained according to *Guinness Book of World Records*) and weigh 418 pounds.

Cliff Dwellers: Located just outside the Anthropology Building, the home of the cliff and cave dwellers was shown in an artificial mountain modeled after Battle Rock in Colorado. Ingenious illusions inside the mountain convinced viewers they were climbing among the rock people.

Indian Exhibit: Displays of Native North Americans were shown, including encampments and items from tribes such as the Cree, Haida, Fort Rupert, Iroquois, Chippewa, Sioux, Menominee, Winnebago, Apache and Navajo.

Peary Relics: A collection of the boats, tents, ropes, clothing and imple-

ments brought back as souvenirs by Robert Peary from his exploration of the Arctic.

Mound Builders: Many states contributed to this display of prehistoric civilizations from mound excavations throughout the country.

Prison Exhibit: Called the most "gruesome" of exhibits, this comprehensive exposé of the devices and methods used for inflicting punishment from the beginning of history through 1893 included the dungeons of the Inquisition, the torture chambers of Oriental barbarism and the Nuremberg collection of old-time instruments of torture. The modern devices of rope, axe and even the electric chair were on display.

Electricity Building

The United States dominated this hall, most notably with exhibits from all of the great electrical companies, telegraph and telephone companies, street, railway and machinery companies. France and Germany, recognized world leaders in electrical inventions, were also well represented. Among the showy exhibits from the latter was its brilliant and startling lighting for stage effects. Throughout the hall, every type of electrical apparatus and process, from motors and appliances to elevators and fire alarms to switchboards and surgical procedures, was shown. There were dynamos, incandescent lighting apparatus, generators, wires, Edison's streetcar motor, phonograph and myriad other electrical inventions, mining hoists, electric drills, switchboards, batteries, fans, cable twisting machines and more. Of course all of the elec-

American Bell Telephone sponsored a large pavilion in the Electricity Building. It showed photographs, charts and maps tracing the company's history, telephones dating to Bell's original version built in 1875, the first microphone, operators at a switchboard and even a long-distance telephone connecting the fair with New York City.

trical displays were considered revolutionary in light of the relatively recent development of electricity.

Earthquake Laboratory: Of particular interest to Japanese visitors and others who lived in fear of earthquakes, this display featured the first seismograph ever invented—dating to the first century—and photographs of the damage wreaked by earthquakes around the world during the nineteenth century.

First Telegraph Message: Western Union displayed the first telegraph message ever sent. The message was received by Professor Morse at the capitol in Washington, D.C. in May 1844 from his assistant in Annapolis. Near this exhibit, the Baltimore & Ohio Railroad Company showed a model of the first telegraph wire strung along its rail line by Morse.

Illuminations: One of the most spectacular things about the Electricity Building was that it powered 100,000 incandescent lamps placed about the fairgrounds and buildings and 10,000 arc lamps used to illuminate the architecture, landscape and glorious fountains. The resulting scene was magical to sightseers.

Kinetoscope: Most fairgoers couldn't believe their eyes—or ears—when they encountered Thomas Edison's most recent invention. This precursor to

Westinghouse Electric received a coveted spot in the central aisle of the Electricity Building.

The Electricity Building was a mass of bright lights and electrical showpieces. American companies shone, with displays by many companies that are still leaders in their field today. In the center of General Electric's exhibit was Edison's "Tower of Light," its shaft encircled by thousands of miniature lamps producing a kaleidoscopic effect.

the movie camera "transmitted scenes to the eye as well as sounds to the ear."

Tower of Light: Another Edison attraction was an 82-foot tower, strung with 18,000 lamps, which gave "bursts of condensed sunlight" when illuminated.

Fine Arts (Palace of)

From nearly 200,000 square feet of canvas displayed in this building the faces and passions, lives, sorrows, fancies, tragedies, romances and realities of the centuries peered down on visitors. America and nearly every European country contributed its most precious paintings for this exhibit. In addition to oil paintings, watercolors, paintings on ivory, enamel, metal and porcelain, there were fresco paintings, engravings and etchings, prints, chalk,

The Palace of Fine Arts housed an extensive array of sculpture, in every material from marble to bronze.

"A Wedding in Little Russia" was among the many Russian paintings that hung in the Palace of Fine Arts. Fairgoers learned more about the fascinating rituals of Russian weddings in the songs and ceremonies performed by the Lineff Russian Choir during several weeks of the exposition.

charcoal, pastel and other drawings; antique and modern carvings; engravings in medallions or in gems, cameos and intaglios. There was also extensive sculpture—figures in marble, casts from original works by modern artists and bas-reliefs in marble and bronze. Examples of the world's finest architecture, including plans and drawings, were also displayed.

American Art: This exhibit of works by Americans consisted of 500 paintings from New York collections, 139 from Boston, 112 from Philadelphia and 75 from Chicago, as well as 140 from Paris, 50 from London, 40 from Munich and 20 from Rome.

American Select: This was a collection of paintings by foreign artists owned by Americans. Among them were works by Constable, Millet, Corot, Rousseau and Diaz.

Foreign Exhibits: England, France, Germany, Japan, Holland, Russia, Spain, Denmark and Italy were major contributors of paintings by foreign artists.

Japanese Art: Unusual to many Westerners, the Japanese paintings on silk, rich lacquer and bronzes, carved ivory and metal work, detailed wood carvings and inlaid work were popular attractions.

A Culinary Carnival

The World's Columbian Exposition engaged more than just the mind and eye. New sounds assaulted the ear at every corner: African drumming, the creak of metallic joints in the Ferris Wheel, and the constant blare of contraptions called phonographs. Smells were all-pervasive, from the fresh, humid breeze off Lake Michigan to the earthy odor of animals in the stock pens.

As one fairgoer observed, all this walking, talking, peering, thinking and exploring inevitably brought on "nervous excitation and a mighty uprising of the soul: it all required blood, and blood required nourishment." The organizers of the exposition believed that four out of every five visitors would want a meal on the fairgrounds, and so they erected establishments capable altogether of serving 17,000 people at one sitting. Fifty cattle were slaughtered every morning to feed the hordes. Trainloads of tropical fruits and other "out of season" foodstuffs arrived daily to keep the agricultural displays fresh, appealing and a source of pride to the exhibitors. Oranges had never been so plentiful in the Windy City, and in the face of this abundance, the wholesale prices of fruits and vegetables plummeted to the lowest levels in Chicago history.

Mass consumption of such quantities of food in the superabundance of restaurants the exposition offered reinforced the idea that this world's fair was the "biggest ever on earth." By serving up a bewildering array of culinary delights from all over the world, the fair's promoters sought to out-Europe Europe in terms of sheer number and variety of cuisines.

Much of the food served at the World's Columbian Exposition was American of the most basic kind: boiled meat, potatoes, bread and a sweet desert. The Wellington Catering Company, owners of a posh downtown restaurant, won the concessions monopoly for food at the fair. Their several restaurants, kitchens and storage warehouses covered nine acres of the fairgrounds and employed a staff of 2,000 waiters, cooks and dishwashers.

The Wellington company concessions extended from food and drink to seltzer waters, cigars and ice cream in and around the fairgrounds. In exchange for a promise to turn back twenty-five percent of its gross receipts to the exposition, the company secured as well the right to require all the other restaurants on the fairgrounds to buy their provisions from Wellington.

But it was the uses the other restaurants made of the provisions that made eating at the Columbian exposition such a memorable gastronomic event.

Entering at the far western end of the Midway, the visitor first encountered the Irish Village, where he could sample oatmeal, potatoes, corned beef and freckle bread, all washed down with a complete line of imported ales and stouts. Past Blarney Castle, he could top off the meal with a glass of iced cocoa in Java Village.

The German Village was the next stop, where a French chef set out hearty German meals and an adjacent beer garden featured a small brass band.

Crossing the second canal, the traveler encountered the sounds and smells of the mysterious East. Along the Street of Cairo, vendors hawked hot zelebiah and pita bread. The Persian, Algerian and Tunisian concessions offered cool tropical-fruit drinks and thick, hot coffee. Those with more conventional tastes could slip into the nearby Chinese Tea House or enjoy a cold beer at Conrad Seipp's Brewing Company. Viennese delicacies were a specialty at the Austrian Village and Hungarian beer was served at the Orpheum.

Near the Ferris Wheel, a visitor could watch an authentic Normandy apple press squeeze Jonathans and Spies into juice that sold for two cents a glass. Perhaps even more popular was the *cidre doux* (alcoholic content 2.5%) and *cidre brut* (alcoholic content 4%), sparkling fermentations of apple juice. Under the sign, "Ye Olden Tyme Log Cabin," the visitor could eat heartily on pork and beans and pumpkin pie for 50 cents. But many chose instead to press on, entering the fair proper at 60th Street, where one could sip tea and munch quail on toast amid the gracious surroundings of the roof garden atop the Woman's Building.

To the north lay new delights in the state pavilions: The Louisiana State Pavilion, a replica of an early eighteenth-century Creole home, featured a Southern Kitchen serving opossum stew, Tabasco-laced gumbo, red beans and rice.

Next to California, New York was the biggest exhibitor of American wines. Depending on the season, 150 varietals, from Advance to Zinnia, were shown by 170 growers, along with 101 varieties of apples and numerous kinds of pears, plums, peaches, apricots, strawberries, gooseberries and currants. Nearby, six hives of leather-colored Italian, golden, common black, and Carniolan bees produced 252 pounds of honey during the summer of 1893.

Strolling around the North Pond, the visitor came next to the Café de la Marine, serving "all animals from Water." At the Japanese Tea House one could sip darjeeling served with a wafer, sweetmeats and "elaborate courtesy."

The Swedish Restaurant specialized in traditional Swedish meals, while the Polish Café featured stuffed cabbage and boiled dumplings. The Clam Bake Building served a seemingly endless supply of littlenecks and steamers. The Banquet Hall laid on a sumptuous repast, while the Soda Pavilion poured sodas, siphon spring and mineral waters to sip with peanuts or popcorn.

The Walter Baker, the Van Houten & Zoon and the Blooker Dutch cocoa companies competed to produce the most delectable chocolate concoctions.

In the Agricultural Building Armour and Company demonstrated some of the many items not yet generally known to the modern home: beef tea in bouillon cups, Star hams and condensed-meat pies. Fairbanks Cottolene portrayed the history of cotton and the range of products made from the cottonseed-oil shortening. The Heinz pickle booth gave free samples of their crispy dills, along with bread and butter, lapel pins, and key chains carrying the Heinz logo.

The Ceylon Tea House

Thatcher's Baking Powder served hot, freshly made baking-powder biscuits. Quaker Oats were served all day in the form of hot, steamy muffins. Magic Yeast served loaves of smooth-topped bread, flaky biscuits and rich coffee cakes. Saccharin was explained, promoted and demonstrated in many booths. Exhibitors of condensed milk demonstrated special menus for the invalid or baby.

In the nearby Electricity Building one could discover the beauties of an electric oven, chafing dish, coffeepot or teapot; linger over turkeys roasted in ovens decorated with flowers; or attend any of the thrice-weekly cooking demonstrations on the "science" of electric cooking.

For those who wandered to the southern end of the park, the French Bakery promoted its wares and the customary Gallic boast that theirs was the best bread in Chicago. Just behind the bakery stood the White Horse Inn, a reproduction of the famous English inn at Ipswich, celebrated by Charles Dickens in his *Pickwick Papers*. Under the sign of the trotting horse, the cooking and service were, as one visitor recalled, "severely English."

Besides the many exhibits featuring food samples, and the restaurants serving complete meals, there were countless vendors selling things to eat, drink and smoke. Popcorn, peanuts, Hygeia water, ice cream and cigars were the most popular.

Crackerjacks, the molasses-covered popcorn-and-peanut concoction, were also introduced at the fair. They are still with us, but few other traces survive the culinary diversity that burst forth at the World's Columbian Exposition.

But for the thousands of visitors, the food became an essential part of their experience. The late nineteenth-century fascination with ethnology and race was satisfied in part by eating the ethnic foods served at the fair. Eating a meal of chapati and yogurt may have made a stronger, more memorable impression than hours of reading about Middle Eastern customs. Even a casual glance at someone quaffing thick-foamed beer would have told more about real people than listening to barbershop gossip. Food at the fair was the basic, international language in which everyone could be fluent. It served to awaken ideas of national and international bonds in a manner every person could understand and it was, perhaps, the perfect learning tool precisely because it came as naturally as swallowing.

—Mary Steffek Blaske, *World's Fair*, Summer 1982

Trocadero Collection: This was a collection of casts used in the reproductions of monumental works in the Palace of the Trocadero in Paris. Some of the casts were enormous. The one for the facade from the Church of St. Gilles was forty-one feet long, twenty-four feet high and eighteen feet wide. Another, from the portal of the Virgin of Notre Dame, was twenty-four feet high.

Fisheries Building

Photographic History of the World's Fair, 1893, described the contents of this building as follows: "Everything that science has rescued from the depths of ocean, sea, lake or river, is displayed.... Inhabitants of deep-sea grottoes; the coral animal, builder of islands; sea anemones that blossom miles below the surface of the ocean; monstrous devil-fish, sharks and other terrors of the deep are seen beside the speckled beauties of stream or lake, the plebeian catfish, perch and sucker, suggest of the boyish angler and the shallow stream. From ocean depths are brought specimens of subaqueous life so marvelously delicate and so richly beautiful that the microscope will only reveal in part their wondrous beauty. The methods, too, by which the mysteries of the deep are penetrated, the paraphernalia of the United States Fish Commission, the wonderful progress made in the art of fish farming, in addition to the implements of commercial fishing and the latest tackle for angling."

Forestry Building

In the late nineteenth century forest land was already well established as a key national resource, and all states and territories of the United States participated in this building. Displays centered around types of trees—all 425 species native to the United States were represented—and wood processing and logging techniques and tools. Surprisingly, concerns about depleting the natural resource were also mentioned and progressive governmental forest management plans were announced at the exposition. Nearly every state erected a pavilion made of its finest native woods.

Displays also featured every imaginable wood product. There was furniture from Grand Rapids, brush handles and wainscoting from West Virginia, the world's largest petrified log from Oregon, a mammoth redwood wine tank from San Francisco, a pulp and paper exhibit from Chicago, a huge log of black walnut from North Carolina, 500 varieties of medicinal herbs from Ohio and a logging camp from Michigan. Foreign countries also made a major showing with such wonders as willow baskets from France, huge blocks of mahogany from Mexico, exquisite woods and dyestuffs from Honduras and Haiti, 321 varieties of timber (each one meter high) from Paraguay, beautiful carved teak from the Middle East and carved temples from Siam.

Horticultural Building

Featuring more than five acres of rare plants and flowers, the choicest fruits and vegetables, and an entire pavilion devoted to viticulture, this hall captured the hearts of the world's gardeners and wine-lovers. Fairgoers could wander through an artistic Japanese garden, a German wine cellar, a Mexi-

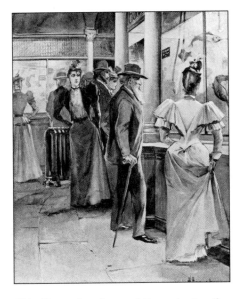

This illustration shows visitors viewing the ever-changing display of marine life in the aquariums housed in the cool, circular arcade of the Fisheries Building.

can desert, a tropical paradise, a field of snap-dragons and other insect-devouring plants, or a sea of pansies. Displays featured wines, fruits, flowers and vegetables in all stages of development. There were fresh, dried, preserved and canned fruits and vegetables. There were mills and presses, and the latest inventions for preserving foods.

Illinois sent exquisite specimens of bay laurels and luscious strawberries. Indiana sent a flourishing field of begonias. Austria's tree ferns rose forty feet or more and its staghorn ferns were eight feet in diameter. Mississippi and Georgia sent mammoth watermelons. New York displayed a large model of the national capitol constructed of Canadian thistles. New Jersey presented a

Los Angeles presented one of the most ostentatious displays of fruit: a thirty-five-foot-high tower of 14,000 oranges. The tower was replenished with fresh oranges every three to four weeks.

profuse display of orchids and ferns. Colorado sent "berries as bright and fresh as her own mountain air" and Idaho showed how grapes, prunes, eggplant and other fruits and vegetables could be grown 6,000 feet above sea level.

In the viticulture section there was everything from sparkling champagnes to Spanish sherries (many, of course, displayed in pyramids). Every wine, port, sherry, brandy and other liqueur imaginable was represented. There were also photographs, books and appliances relating to the management of vineyards, and the manufacture, bottling, packing and shipping of food products.

Flower Gardens: Ten of the sixteen acres on Wooded Island were planted in flowers, including a gorgeous rose garden. Half a million pansies, 100,000 roses and millions of other flowers were also on display. (There was even 20,000 feet of space devoted to flower seeds!)

Oregon Preserves: This was a beautiful display of three-foot-high jars containing pears weighing as much as four pounds each. The state also regularly shipped in a fresh display of cherries, berries, apples, peaches and plums.

The world's greatest dynamo was displayed in the Intramural Railroad Company building at the south end of the exposition grounds. The caption given in The Columbian Gallery, *an 1893 book, explained the dynamo best: "When it is considered that this railroad is six and a half miles long, has sixteen trains of cars in constant movement and this aggregate of sixty-four cars [is] frequently crowded with passengers, some idea may be formed of the energy sent forth by this revolving giant. It may be desirable to many, however, to know just what an electric dynamo is. In 1864, thirty years ago, the Italian Pacinotti described in a scientific journal an 'electro magnetic machine,' and said it could be used to generate electricity by applying power to revolve the armature. Nothing came of it at the time, but in 1873, at the Vienna Exposition, somebody accidentally picked up and attached to the terminals of an electro-magnetic machine the ends of two wires which were lying on the ground. These two wires happened at that moment to be attached to another similar machine that was running by steam power. The idle machine began to move like the other. Then became known what very strangely was not known before, or revealed by investigations, and the revolutionary twins were born, the dynamo and the motor, which together are changing the aspect of the civilized world."*

The grand section of Machinery Hall assaulted fairgoers' ears with the clanking and grinding of its mechanical wonders. It featured everything from engines and boilers to sewing machines and bathtub heaters. Although the displays were interesting, the noise was almost unbearable and most spectators did not linger long inside.

Orchids: More than 16,000 varieties of orchids, valued at several hundred thousand dollars, were displayed beneath the glass roof of the Horticultural Building.

Palm Mountain: Just inside the main portal was a collection of plants from nearly every climate in the world, arranged around huge palms and cacti. At the base of the mountain was a huge cavern, studded with crystals from South Dakota.

Tower of Oranges: The Southern California Fair Association erected a thirty-five-foot-high, five-foot-diameter tower of navel oranges topped by a stuffed eagle. Visitors who guessed the number of oranges in the display won a box of oranges.

Machinery Hall

A mechanic's mecca, this building featured examples of every type of mechanical device known to man. Among the many displays were motors, engines, boilers, pumps, fire-fighting apparatus, machinists' tools, forging and metal-working tools, and mechanical processes used in printing. There was machinery for working minerals, processing food, drying cotton, cutting wood, operating fountains, hoisting engines, making fabric, drawing beer and bottling beer, knitting, weaving, washing clothes, setting type, cutting metal, purifying water, making bricks,

heating bathtubs, drilling for oil, refrigerating food, making boxes, stitching books and more.

Cotton Gin: The first cotton gin made by Eli Whitney was exhibited by the New Orleans Machinery Company, along with an array of other cotton gins and sugar machinery.

Largest Belt: A New Hampshire company displayed the largest conveyor belt in the world. It took 569 hides to create the 200-foot-long, eight-and-a-half-foot-wide, 5,176-pound belt.

Power Plant: Here were forty-three steam engines, each with 18,000 to 20,000 horsepower, that operated 127 dynamos, which in turn produced electric light and power for all of the buildings at the exposition. Twelve engines powered Machinery Hall alone.

Sewing Machines: Among the sewing machines exhibited was one designed for carpets. To demonstrate, an operator would ride a velocipede along for 100 feet, guiding an electric motor which in turn powered the moving sewing machine and stitched the carpet on 100-foot lengths.

Weighing Machines: Here, fairgoers were amazed to see a machine that packaged several tons of coffee a day. It took a pound of coffee from a hopper, poured it into a bag, and sealed it in a matter of seconds.

Germany's whimsical stagecoach, with very real-looking passengers, was a big attraction with children in the Manufactures and Liberal Arts Building.

THE WORLD'S COLUMBIAN EXPOSITION

The Belgian Pavilion in the Manufactures and Liberal Arts Building was built in Belgium, disassembled for shipment to Chicago and re-assembled onsite. The country's most outstanding displays featured furniture with rich upholstery and intricate carvings, ceramics, bronze works and plate glass.

Manufactures and Liberal Arts Building

As the largest of the Great Buildings by far, this department housed the greatest number of exhibits on the fairgrounds. There were more participants in this building than at the entire Philadelphia Centennial Exposition in 1876. The categories of displays alone numbered in the hundreds, from chemical and pharmaceutical products to clothing and travel gear to coffins and soaps, ceramics and flatware, the list goes on. There were scientific instruments, medical supplies and even a collection of all known bacteria. It is safe to say that every type of product ever created for use by men and women was represented in the manufactures section.

In the Liberal Arts Department, also located in this hall, there were 70,000 square feet devoted to musical instruments, extensive university displays on

Elevators such as this one displayed by Otis-Hale Company in the Manufactures and Liberal Arts Building were quite a fascination in 1893.

The Tiffany & Co. display was one of the most valuable presented at the exposition.

France presented a particularly beautiful display of statuary. This life-size Guardian Spirit of the Secret of the Tomb *is a bronze copy of a work by Parisian sculptor St. Marceau. When the sculpture first appeared in a show in France in the early 1890s, it reportedly took the art world by storm.*

all aspects of research and education, church displays, technical and parochial school exhibits, photography exhibits and priceless books and manuscripts.

Composers' Instruments: Here were Bach's clavichord, Mozart's spinet; Beethoven's grand piano of six and a half octaves and Haydn's piano in a white oaken case.

Niagara: This old gunboat, which was sunk in Massasauga Bay in Erie Harbor in the War of 1812, was displayed.

'Poem of the Vine': An immense bronze vase, decorated with hundreds of imaginative figures such as cupids, lizards and insects, was displayed by France. The three-ton, thirteen-foot-high creation was designed by Gustave Dore.

Remington Exhibit: In this beautiful mahogany pavilion were exhibited forty typewriters adapted to all languages and purposes, including English, French, German, Spanish, Portuguese, Russian, Hungarian, Italian and Swedish for mathematical, medical, billing and weather-bureau operations. Also shown here was the first Columbian half dollar struck for the fair, for which the Remington Company paid $10,000.

Stained Glass Exhibit: A brilliantly colored depiction of Christ explain-

The Yerkes telescope, exhibited on Columbia Avenue in the Manufactures and Liberal Arts Building, was the largest telescope in the world. After the fair, it was rescued from a fire that raged through the Court of Honor in 1894. The telescope was then given to the University of Chicago observatory in Williams Bay, Wisconsin.

Nearly all leading English and Irish manufacturers participated in England's displays in the Manufactures and Liberal Arts Building. One of the highlights was a magnificent silver tea caddy, c. 1792, which included a lock and key. Another was Irish linen. One of the novel displays was the Shakespearean casket, which illustrated in gold and silver the great works of the poet and playwright.

ing the Trinity was contributed by the Continental Stained Glass Company of Boston.

Tiffany Exhibit: A beautiful pavilion housed the most costly display of jewelry and precious stones ever exhibited.

University Exhibits: Nearly every American university exhibited in the liberal arts section. Their contributions included curricula, model libraries, model classrooms, teacher training manuals, photographs of famous professors, diplomas, awards, and even menus.

Yerkes Telescope: The $500,000 telescope presented to the University of Chicago by millionaire Charles Yerkes, was sixty-five feet in length and weighed seventy tons.

Mines and Mining Building

Every state and foreign nation with an interest in mining featured a display in this building. Most common were huge pyramids or other structures built of pure ore and replicas of mining operations. All of the treasures of the earth, in minerals and ores, gems and precious stones, building stone and coal, clays and salts, were displayed. The history of mining and the methods used by different nations to extract and process ore, from the earliest ages on, were shown again and again in interesting exhibits.

Diamond Exhibit: Under heavy security, this display by the Kimberly Diamond Mining Company of South Africa featured great quantities of diamond dust and prized gems.

New South Wales presented a magnificent display of silver-bearing ores at its exhibit in the Mines and Mining Building.

Foote Collection: This was recognized as one of the finest private collections of mineralogy in the world.

Grecian Exhibit: This was a small display of many relics and tools used by the Greeks thirty centuries earlier in primitive mining operations.

Michigan: This state's display included two masses of copper ore weighing 6,200 pounds and 8,500 pounds respectively. Also featured was a miniature model of the largest copper mine and reducing mills in the world.

Montana: This pavilion featured a silver statue of American actress Ada Rehan, chosen because of "the grace and symmetry of her form."

Silver Queen: The heroic figure of a girl of seventeen, the same age as the state of Colorado, was cast in silver and featured in the state's display.

Statue of Liberty in Salt: A five-foot six-inch replica of the *Statue of Liberty* was carved out of a block of salt unearthed from a depth of 250 feet.

Transportation Building

Considered one of the most interesting buildings of the fair, both in its architecture and contents, this hall included every vehicle known to man, ranging from a baby carriage to a rail dining car. Row after row of displays

Though it may not have received much attention in the Transportation Building, the sedan chair became a familiar site as it taxied people around the grounds (right). One reporter described this Turkish village concession as follows: "For the first few weeks of the fair's existence the sedan chairs had little patronage; but they are gradually increasing in favor. Their tops protect their occupants from the sun, and the slight motion produced by the steady trot of the bearers is much pleasanter, when one becomes accustomed to it, than the jostling of the ordinary wheeled chairs of the exposition grounds (below), which, with their student attendants, have thus far proved dangerous rivals of the Oriental conveyances in the favor of a conservative public." The sedan chair cost seventy-five cents per hour; the wheeled chair was seventy-five cents per hour with attendant, forty cents without.

The Exhibits and Attractions

showed models of every type of nautical craft, a Roman galley, a Chinese junk, Fulton's first engine, African bullock carts, Aboriginal canoes, Chinese sedan chairs, Japanese rickshaws, Indian howdahs, Arabian camels and even pneumatic cash carriers.

Bicycle Exhibit: Every type and size of this increasingly popular mode of transportation, from a forty-pound roadster to a seventeen-pound racer, embracing tandems, triplets, solid, cushion and pneumatic tires, forgings, bearing cases and balls, and so on, was shown here.

English Warships: This exhibit featured the latest-model ships of the British Navy.

Great Trip Hammer: This 125-ton hammer, exhibited by Bethlehem Iron Works, was a replica of the company's massive tool used to forge heavy iron and steel work, including the axle of the fair's Ferris Wheel.

Historical Wagon: A 150-year-old wagon which had belonged to a first-generation Connecticut family was displayed.

Locomotive Exhibit: "John Bull," the first locomotive ever run in America, and full-size models of the ten oldest railroad locomotives in the world, were big draws.

North German Lloyd Exhibit: Located in the center of the Transportation Building was a large map of the world on which the daily positions of all vessels of this huge steamship line were placed.

Railroad Relics: This display included a set of the circular tickets used on the first train run on the Philadelphia & Reading line and a copy of the

The ancient state carriage of Dom Pedro, the first emperor of Brazil, for some unknown reason was displayed among the relics of American transportation.

official notice announcing opening of the same line. Other domestic and international contributions included original tickets, passes, passenger way bills and workers' time cards.

Steamships: Two hundred models of steamships that had been or were in use by England's famed Peninsula & Oriental Company were on display. All of the great transatlantic steamship companies also exhibited, key among them the White Star line which actually built its own display building for the exposition. Also exhibited was a model of the cruiser *Alabama*, built in England for the Confederate government.

Strange and Unusual: Among the more novel items were a sled of spruce with runners made from the jawbone of a whale from Unalakleet; a set of snowshoes without netting used on hard-packed snow; a toboggan made of birch and held together with thongs of reindeer hide, two Turkish rowing boats, a rolling hogshead used 200 years earlier to deliver tobacco to market in Virginia, and an ancient chariot from the Etruscan museum in Florence, Italy.

U.S. Government Building

This building featured many fine antiquities such as a Bible printed in 1559, a fragment of Plymouth Rock, Benedict Arnold's fife, pitch-pipes used

The Smithsonian Institution and National Museum's displays in the U.S. Government Building were lauded for their meticulous labeling and organization. Their displays on physical geology included studies of volcanoes, glaciers, caves and minerals, while the natural history exhibits included a complete collection of American fauna and a ranking of the animal kingdom from the monkey at the highest level to the opossum at the lowest. Nearly every animal, insect, bird and reptile imaginable was displayed in life-size forms carefully prepared by skilled taxidermists.

by Puritans, bronzes made by Paul Revere and John Hancock's ring. All major federal departments presented displays, among them calculating machines from the Census Department; coins, currency, engravings and an operating mint from the Treasury Department; stamp collections, a model post office, mailbags and dead letter files from the Post Office; historic documents from the State Department; models of all the warships from the U.S. Navy; all types of military displays from the War Department; and original models of American inventions from the Patent Office, to name a few.

One of many postcards and trade cards spawned by the exposition

California Big Tree: The trunk of the mammoth "Big Tree" of California could be entered from the floor beneath the building's dome.

Carrier Pigeons: These birds amazed visitors as they traveled up to 200 miles from the exposition grounds.

Currency Display: The Registry Office exhibited 640 samples of currency, representing every piece of paper money ever issued by the U.S. government.

Dead Letter Exhibit: A curious display of all the odd items retrieved from the Post Office's dead letter file included snakes, stuffed elephants, tambourines, coffee pots, roller skates, Chinese shoes, accordions and circular saws.

First Typewriter: Invented in 1823, the original typewriter had been destroyed in a U.S. Patent Office fire in 1836, but a model had been recreated for the fair, using descriptions found in old patent documents signed by Andrew Jackson.

California's giant Sequoia or "Big Tree" was a big attraction. Fairgoers could walk through it in the U.S. Government Building or drink upon it at the Big Tree Restaurant.

Old veterans who attended the fair most likely got a charge out of this display of Uncle Sam's "Corps of Kickers."

Ocean Currents: For this display the surface of the earth was laid out on a thirty-foot-square model onto which pipes pumped water simulating ocean currents.

Officers in Uniform: The War Department exhibited models of Army officers of all grades, mounted, on foot, fully equipped in the uniform of their rank and service from all significant wars in American history.

Postage Stamps: This was the most extensive display of postage stamps ever exhibited in one place, contributed by the American Philatelic Association. Several of the stamps were valued at $1,000 each.

Torpedo: The War Department exhibited the largest torpedo owned by the United States, the twenty-five-foot-long Sims-Edison torpedo.

Woman's Building

This building was designed by a woman, managed by women, and devoted to the exhibition of women's work in every field, from arts and sciences, to learned professions, to handicraft and philanthropic endeavors. Displays included paintings, sculpture, engravings, photography, china painting techniques, stained glass windows, Bohemian embroideries, musical compositions, lacework, scientific works, patented technological inventions (including washing machines, refrigerators, dusters, flour sifters, egg beaters, meat

The Casino at the Lake Michigan entrance to the fair was one of the many facilities catering to the not-so-adventuresome visitor hungering for a good ol' American meal of meat and potatoes.

boilers, beef manglers, frying pans, surgical bandages, hot-water appliances and sanitary dinner pails), books, cooking schools, homemaking and childcare centers—all created by women throughout the world.

Among the highlights were books that have become the Biblioteca Femina at Northwestern University; a rare manuscript of *Jane Eyre*, written in Charlotte Brontë's own hand and a copy of an 1879 law allowing women lawyers to plead cases before the U.S. Supreme Court.

African Curios: A large collection of curios brought back by adventurer May French Sheldon from her African safari made an exciting exhibit.

Cassatt and MacMonnies Murals: The works of impressionist painter Mary Cassatt were not well-known in 1893. The Women's Department recognized her talent and that of Mrs. Frederick MacMonnies' by hanging their works, *Modern Woman* and *Primitive Woman*, respectively, in the building.

Costumes: Seventeen French dolls dressed in the prevailing fashions of different periods in American history, beginning in 1565, were displayed.

Kentucky Home: An old colonial home was meticulously created and decorated with priceless Kentucky antiques.

"Women in Savagery": This display included artifacts from the hands of primitive women.

Auxiliary Buildings

Whether strolling or hurrying through the grounds, visitors couldn't help but see the numerous large and small buildings, pavilions, kiosks, cafes and other attractions scattered among the Great Buildings. Although the latter dominated the skyline, the so-called Auxiliary Buildings were often equally as beautiful on the exterior and compelling on the interior. Following is a look at what some of these attractions offered.

Casino

At the end of the dock where fairgoers arrived by steamer was the Casino, a three-story Renaissance-style structure with Corinthian columns. Designed entirely for "the comfort of visitors," the ground floor featured luxurious

The Brazilian Café was a favorite spot for steaming rich coffee and a good view of passersby—though one would never know it from the somber faces in this photo.

sofas and easy chairs, parlors, lavatories and smoking rooms, and the second floor featured a massive American restaurant equipped to serve 1,500 people "all the good things to eat of this continent" at a reasonable price. One cafe was intended for women only, one for women escorted by men and another for gentlemen only.

Children's Building

Though most cities today abound with entertainment for children, from amusement parks to video games to roller rinks, the nineteenth-century child was lucky to find a park to romp in. Children and parents alike attending the World's Columbian Exposition were thrilled to find the Children's Building.

Charming statues of children adorned the grounds. Inside, the walls were decorated with colorful murals of heart-warming scenes from Grimm's fairy tales. From floor to ceiling were displays of every type of toy known to civilization, contributed by nearly every country in the world. France, considered a leader in toy-making ingenuity, exhibited such curious contrivances as "toy men who performed almost human feats of skill . . . and toy animals invested with the intelligence of trained domestic beasts." Russia, Germany, Sweden, Norway and Japan also sponsored extensive exhibits.

There were many hands-on opportunities, including a complete gymnasium located in the center of the main floor. One popular attraction was the "kitchen garden," a room devoted to teaching little girls how to become good housewives. Here forty kindergartners demonstrated how to make beds, sweep floors, set the table, scrub clothes and sit down demurely. Another hit

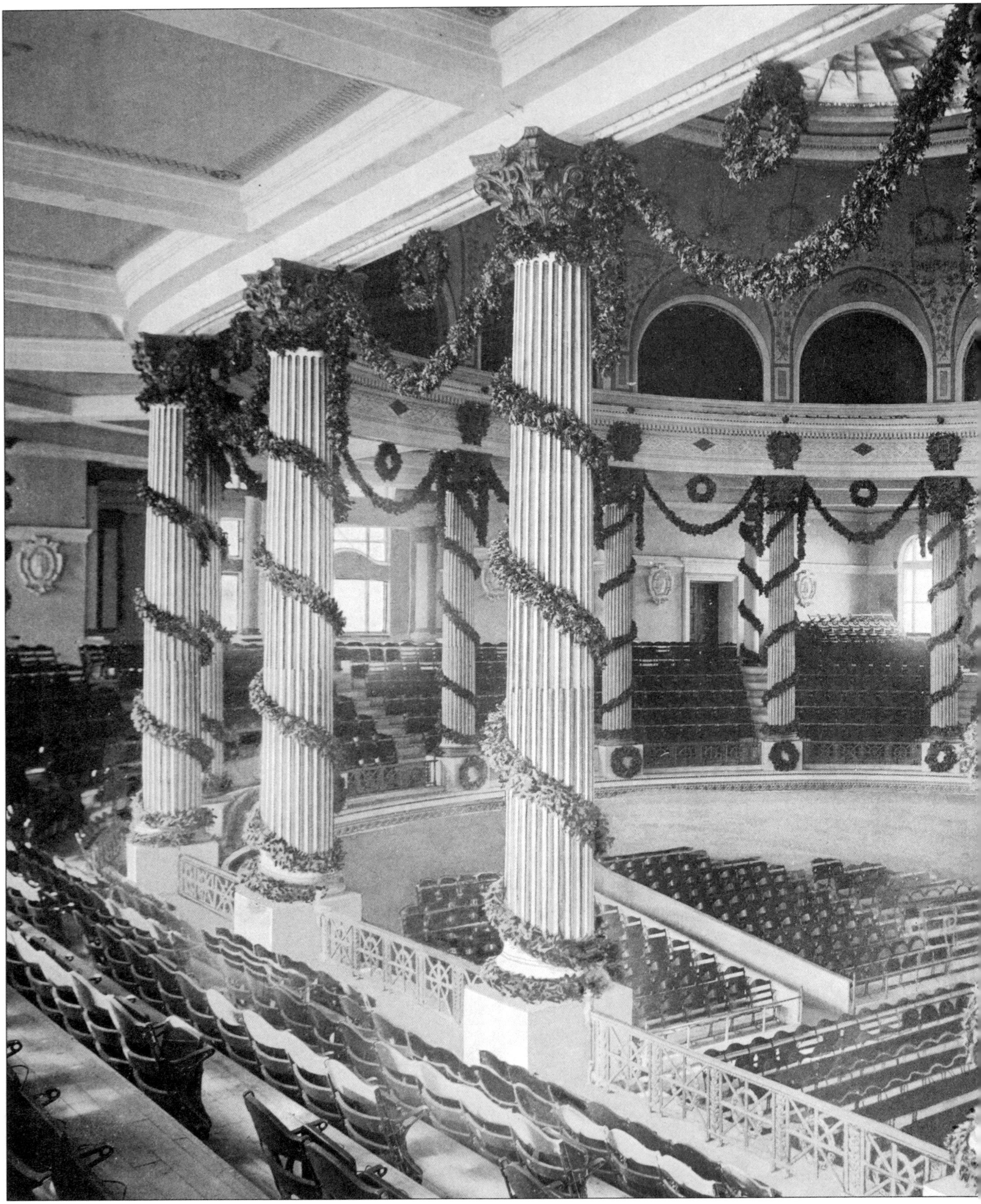

Choral Hall, with its 2,500-person choir in a lavish amphitheater, lured music lovers from around the world.

Christopher Columbus' humble caravels, including the Santa Maria pictured here, were reproduced to the most precise detail in Spain and sailed to America for the Columbian exposition. Although it is difficult to see in the above photograph, the Santa Maria's decks are crowded with fair visitors.

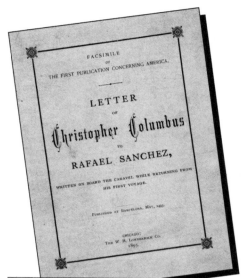

The Monastery of La Rabida, a replica of the structure in Palos, Spain, where Columbus stayed before setting sail on his famous voyage, featured wonderful displays of the voyager's memorabilia, including a copy of his first correspondence about America.

was a Swedish workshop where boys could handle carpentry tools and learn woodcarving techniques.

The building also contained model classrooms and displays of educational materials. One of the most interesting rooms was devoted to demonstrating the latest methods for teaching deaf children how to communicate.

Much to the relief of weary parents—and irritable children—the building also offered day care for babies and children. Parents could leave their children with attentive nannies for an hourly fee while they attended lectures on education and child-rearing or continued their tour of other buildings. This is one area in which the exposition had severely underestimated the crowds: Hundreds of babies were turned away each day.

Best of all, at least as far as most children were concerned, was the rooftop playground. A grassy yard, filled with flowers, arbors, birds and butterflies, awaited visiting children. They could float boats in the basin of a large fountain, fly kites in the brisk Chicago winds, play any of an assortment of games, read books or join in a round of leap-frog.

Choral Hall

Those whose musical interests leaned toward vocals, could take a seat in beautiful Choral Hall to hear any number of daily performances by a 2,500-person choir.

Columbus' Caravels

Full-size replicas of the *Nina*, the *Pinta* and the *Santa Maria*, painstakingly accurate in every detail, were built in Spain under the supervision of the Spanish government and navy and sailed to Chicago for the exposition.

The caravels were moored in the South Pond, near the Agricultural Building, where fairgoers could climb aboard and see that even the interiors were outfitted exactly as the originals—stifling in their small size and sparse in amenities.

Dairy Pavilion

This half-acre building featured a dairy school, butter and other product exhibits, 2,500 square feet devoted to a model dairy in operation and studies on various breeds of dairy cows.

Hunter's Cabin

Also known as the Davy Crockett Cabin, this hut on a small island just south of Wooded Island was a sharp contrast to the stately buildings that loomed across the lagoon. Filled with Crockett relics and hunting and trapping gear, the cabin was sponsored by the Boone and Crockett Foundation, which was headed by Theodore Roosevelt.

Japanese Ho-o-den

On the north end of Wooded Island was Japan's Ho-o-den, a collection of three buildings representing Japanese architectural styles of the twelfth, sixteenth and eighteenth centuries. The buildings were connected in such a way as to form the shape of a Ho-o, a mythical Japanese bird that could not be destroyed by fire.

Krupp Gun Exhibit

Arms and artillery were displayed extensively throughout various buildings, but the most popular display was in the Krupp Gun Pavilion, located south of the Casino. The centerpiece of the $500,000 exhibit, sent from the well-known Krupp Gun Company in Essen, Germany, was the largest and most powerful gun ever cast. Weighing 127 tons, the monster weapon mea-

Hunter's Cabin, a log house with clay floor and stick chimney, was built to honor Daniel Boone and Davy Crockett.

Bandstands like this one near Machinery Hall dotted the grounds of the Court of Honor and lined the walkway between the Manufactures and Liberal Arts Building and Lake Michigan. Performers from around the world reserved space to play for the crowds attending the fair.

Special Admission Fees

Within the Exposition

Service or Attraction		Cost
Cliff Dwellers' Exhibit	$	.25
Crystal Cave, Horticultural Building		.10
Elevator to Roof, Manufactures Building		.25
Elevators, Transportation Building		.10
Eskimo Village		.25
French Cider Press		.10
Movable Sidewalk, Round Trip		.10
Nippon Tea House, Wooded Island		.10–.50
World's Fair Steamship, Round Trip		.25

Midway Plaisance

Service or Attraction		Cost
Algerian and Tunisian Village	$	.25
American Indian Village		.25
Austrian Village—Old Vienna		.25
Bernese Alps Electric Theatre		.10
Cairo Street		
Egyptian Temple		.25
Street Performances		.25
Camel Rides		.50
Donkey Rides		.25
California Ostrich Farm		.10
Captive Balloon		
Viewing		.25
Ride		2.00
Chinese Village		.25
Costumed Natives		.25

Service or Attraction		Cost
Dahomey Village	$	.25
Diving Bell Exhibit		.10
Dutch East India Village		.25
Eiffel Tower Model		.25
Ferris Wheel, two round trips		.50
German Village, Museum		.15–.25
Hagenbeck's		
Amphitheater		.25–1.00
Zoological Arena		.25
Hungarian Concert Pavilion		.25
Irish Village, with Natives		
(Includes Privilege of Kissing Blarney Stone)		.25
Kilauea Panorama		.50
Laplander Village		.25
Moorish Palace		.10–.25
Natatorium, with Baths		.25–.50
Persian Building		.50
South Sea Islanders Village		.10–.25
St. Peter's Cathedral		.25
Turkish Village		.50–.75
Persian Tent		.25
Sedan Chairs		.75
Street Scene		.50
Syrian Photos		.25
Tribe of Bedouins		.25
Venice-Murano Exhibit		.25
Wheeled Chairs, with attendant		.75

—The Best Things at the World's Fair, 1893

sured 57 feet from breech to muzzle. Although Krupp could not demonstrate the gun's full range of sixteen miles, it did display the huge eighteen-inch-thick steel targets that had been pummeled by the gun's ammunition. After the fair, Krupp donated the gun to the city of Chicago.

Germany's Krupp Gun Company erected an enormous building in which to display its arms and artillery.

Libbey Glass

The Libbey Glass Company of Toledo, Ohio, operated one of the most popular concessions at the fair. Thousands of visitors each day viewed the 100 or more glass-making processes demonstrated here. Many onlookers purchased the bottles, vases and George Washington hatchets offered as souvenirs. Admission was a dime, refundable with a purchase.

Lighthouse

A working lighthouse, one hundred feet high with a massive, state-of-the-art revolving light, was displayed on the lakefront near the replica battleship *Illinois*.

MacMonnies Fountain *and* Statue of the Republic

Perhaps the most striking pieces of statuary at the exposition were the magnificent *MacMonnies Fountain*, named for its designer, Frederick MacMonnies (although it was also called the *Columbian Fountain*), and the *Statue of the Republic*, often called *Columbia*, designed by Daniel Chester French. The two great works faced each other from opposite ends of the Grand Basin.

The centerpiece of the fountain, on the west end of the basin, was a

GOOD FOR 15 CENTS

To apply upon a purchase. Two
or more tickets cannot apply on the
same article.

LIBBEY GLASS CO.
(OVER)

*The Libbey Glass concession was a popular
stop for souvenir seekers who could buy
any number of beautiful glass renderings,
from paperweights to hatchets.*

Ship of State, represented by a triumphal barge. The barge was attended by
eight sea horses, each ridden by youthful figures. The barge itself was rowed
by eight female figures representing various disciplines of the arts and sciences. At the helm was a figure of *Time*. All of the figures were at least twelve
feet high. When illuminated at night, the fountain's myriad jets sprayed rain-
bows of water in dancing patterns to a height of 150 feet.

On the opposite end of the Grand Basin, in front of the Peristyle, the
magnificent *Statue of the Republic* rose from a platform in the water to a heroic height of sixty-five feet.

Like so much of the fair, this stunning statuary gave a misleading appearance of permanence, as if standing guard over the fair. But like most of
the other structures, the statues were built of staff and intended to last not
much longer than the six-month run of the fair.

Monastery of La Rabida

This was an exact replica of the Franciscan Monastery where an ex-
hausted Columbus took refuge in 1492 prior to receiving an audience with
Queen Isabella in hopes of obtaining financing for his famous voyage. A
variety of fascinating artifacts were displayed, including actual correspondence
from Columbus to Isabella, original Columbus manuscripts, autographs and
documents, copies of more than 100 of the earliest printed books relating to
America, portraits of Columbus and what was said to be the first map of the
world—the Diego Ribere map completed in 1529, loaned by the Vatican Library. Also displayed in the monastery were the relics of the first Christian

church in the western hemisphere, a collection of pictures and documents from the Vatican and, of a more frivolous nature, gold coins made from the first gold found in America.

Music Hall

At the opposite end of the Peristyle from the Casino was the glorious Music Hall, very similar in size and exterior style to the Casino. Here, 2,500 people at a time could hear the 300-piece Columbian orchestra perform a wide variety of productions. Depending on one's tastes and schedule, a visitor could attend Handel's *Messiah*, Beethoven's *Ninth Symphony*, Mozart's *Requiem Mass* or Gounod's *Redemption*.

New England Clam Bake

Here, fairgoers looking for fresh seafood could feast on a delightful selection of clams, lobster, fish and seaweed, along with baked beans "cooked in pure Yankee style." The two-story building was privately constructed and located on the lakefront near the Foreign Buildings. The seafood was brought in daily by refrigerated railcars from New England.

Old Fort Dearborn

The city of Chicago traced its roots to Old Fort Dearborn, the collection of buildings around which the city sprang up. The only remaining building of the original fort was a log structure that had been covered with clapboard and sold for commercial use just prior to the fair. When the boards were removed to prepare the building for display at the exposition, a number of arrowheads, knives and other

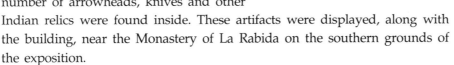

Indian relics were found inside. These artifacts were displayed, along with the building, near the Monastery of La Rabida on the southern grounds of the exposition.

Shoe and Leather Building

This privately funded pavilion, featuring virtually every technique of manufacture involving leather, covered nearly 90,000 square feet. It was located at the southeast corner of the grounds next to the Forestry Building. Here, the traveler could watch skilled craftsmen transform a piece of rawhide into a man's sturdy walking shoe or a woman's dainty slipper.

Stock Pavilion

The 500-foot by 200-foot oval pavilion was used for displays of every type of livestock from cattle to pigs, as well as for competitions. One of the most popular displays was a collection of dogs, including the St. Bernard Lord Bute, reputed to be the biggest dog in the world at thirty-six inches in height and 247 pounds. With seating for 1,500 spectators, the ring was situated near the Agricultural and Machinery buildings.

Norway's Viking ship

Van Houten & Zoon Cocoa Exhibit

This Dutch cocoa manufacturer erected a large building on the lakefront near the Manufactures and Liberal Arts Building. Part of the exhibit was a Cocoa School where Dutch maidens, clad in native attire, mixed and served delicious cocoa beverages.

Viking Ship

The Norwegian government sent an exact replica of the 1,000-year-old vessel commanded by Leif Ericson for display at the exposition. The 76-foot-long vessel was patterned after the original Viking ship, which was purportedly unearthed just four years before the fair was held. The ship was moored at the Naval Pier in Lake Michigan.

State and Foreign Buildings

Visitors who felt pangs of homesickness could head for the northern portion of the grounds where the state and foreign headquarters buildings were located. Here, they could swell with pride (at least in most cases) as

Wisconsin's headquarters, which fronted the North Lagoon, was made of Wisconsin woods, brown stone, granite and terra cotta. A beautiful stained-glass window adorned the second story.

they viewed the building their state or country had erected. Once inside, they could mingle with fellow countrymen or sip a familiar coffee or iced beverage from home.

Every state and territory of the United States was represented in some manner on the fairgrounds. If they could raise the funds, most chose to sponsor a free-standing building, carefully designed and decorated to reflect the character of the state it represented. Many of the buildings were made entirely of materials native to the respective state, whether it was the beautiful wood of the Pacific Northwest or the granite of Vermont. All of the buildings served as a headquarters for state officials and reception hall for residents visiting the fair; some also had displays that highlighted their history, arts, natural resources or industrial accomplishments. But all of the states featured their most extensive exhibits in the Great Buildings.

Through their creative architecture and displays the states did a generally outstanding job of demonstrating their contribution to the country's rich heritage and diversity. Following are highlights of the State Buildings:

Alabama: The centerpiece of this building was a 20,000-square-foot relief map of the state showing major mineral deposits, farming centers and other geographic points of interest.

Arkansas: The focal point of Arkansas' display was a fountain of Hot Springs crystals.

California: One of the largest State Buildings (along with Illinois, New York and Washington), California's headquarters was designed to look like an old mission with ancient Spanish bells in its towers and a rooftop garden. Among its displays were a train carved from a 28-foot by 400-foot Redwood tree; a bird's-eye view of San Francisco; a 127-year-old palm tree rising 100

Unlike most of the State Buildings, California's was full of exhibits as well as functioning as a reception hall. Sacramento County's pavilion (right), lined with glass mirrors to make it appear even larger than its twenty-five- by twenty-five-foot size, featured shelves of jelly and fruit in decorative jars.

feet in the middle of the rotunda; a huge fountain spewing streams of red wine; and a variety of exhibits fashioned entirely of oranges.

Colorado: The building was made of granite and marble. The columns of the building were wrapped with grain, and the frieze was composed of a series of pictures wrought in colored grain. Inside were extensive mineral exhibits; more than 1,000 pressed plants, 200 varieties of fruit molded in wax; 2,000 insects; and a famous statue, *The Last of His Race*, a dying buffalo with an Indian by its side.

Connecticut: Although the state failed to appropriate funds, private citizens raised $50,000 to finance a headquarters and a variety of exhibits in various Great Buildings.

Delaware: True to its relative geographic size, Delaware erected one of the smallest State Buildings, measuring 58 feet by 60 feet. Highlights inside included native timber, local art and historical displays, a Colonial room and church exhibits.

Florida: The building was a one-fifth-scale reproduction of Fort Marion, in St. Augustine, the oldest permanent European settlement in North America, dating to 1620. Its most notable display showcased native gardens and miniature fields of cotton, sugar, rice and tobacco. It also displayed a three-acre flower exhibition in the Horticultural Building.

Georgia: This state erected a modest building that was classical in style, Athenian in form.

Idaho: The building looked like a Swiss chalet, furnished in rustic style and featuring extensive mineral and taxidermy collections.

Illinois: As host to the fair, Illinois was the largest and most favorably located of the State Buildings. The state had appropriated a huge amount in 1893 terms—$800,000, of which $250,000 was spent on the building (made of Illinois brick, stone and steel) and the rest on exhibits. It displayed an enormous fossil collection; Illinois coal; heroic statuary and extensive art exhibits; model classrooms; an immense mosaic of grains and grasses creating the "ideal Illinois prairie farm"; mementos of Gen. Ulysses S. Grant; a landscape composed of native grains and grasses; and the Woman's Corn Kitchen, showing more than 100 different methods for preparing corn.

Indiana: The 6,000-square-foot building featured various local arts and industry exhibits.

Iowa: It displayed a palace made out of corn, modeled after the Iowa State Capitol building; corn of every color and variety hung from the building's central dome.

Kansas: Its building was constructed entirely of materials native to Kansas. Its displays centered on natural history.

Kentucky: Tobacco and distilling displays dominated this state's colonial mansion. A reputation for hospitality made it a popular spot for reunions and receptions. A wonderful collection of stuffed animals and a toy train traveling on a track that ran around the skylight of the building's rotunda delighted adults as well as youngsters.

Louisiana: This state's spacious plantation-style structure housed treasures and mementos of Creole and plantation life, relics of the Spanish and

The rustic elk which stood so conspicuously over the door to Montana's building was a sharp contrast to the Roman arches, pillars and pediments beneath it. Montana focused on its mineral resources in both the inscription on the exterior and the decor of the interior.

French periods, rice and sugar displays, and a special exhibit of schools for black children.

Maine: This small, turreted structure was made of Maine granite, wood and slate, and served primarily as a reception hall with only a few scattered exhibits.

Maryland: The building featured major exhibits on the canning and oyster industries so important to the state, with an elaborate working canned-goods operation.

Massachusetts: A reproduction of John Hancock's house, this building displayed fascinating relics such as copies of charters by King Charles, autographs of Boston poets, books brought to America on the *Mayflower* and colonial furniture.

Michigan: The 40,000-square-foot building, like so many, was built entirely of native materials. It featured a large assembly room and two exhibit halls housing Michigan relics and curiosities.

Minnesota: Described by one guidebook as "one of the handsomest on the grounds," this building was financed by state appropriations and donations from every county in the state. A statue of Hiawatha, financed by collections from Minnesota schoolchildren, stood at the front of the building.

Mississippi: This state's small headquarters was designed to look like a "hospitable" Southern mansion. The state also exhibited in many of the Great Buildings.

Missouri: The "Show Me" state showed them at the exposition with a stately building decorated extravagantly with lace curtains and wallpaper studded with minerals. Its displays of agriculture and mineral endeavors were extensive.

Montana: This "young but wealthy" state built a structure that looked like a small clubhouse. Inside were a relief map of a Butte mining camp and mining tools and artifacts, but its most impressive exhibit—thirty-five tons of minerals, including a life-size statue of a woman in silver—was featured in the Mines and Mining Building.

Nebraska: This building encompassed 10,000 square feet, including an attractive veranda, which overlooked a small lake. The state displayed a variety of agricultural items, and a newspaper exhibit featuring "ancient" papers as well as contemporary, which attracted many newsmen covering the fair.

New Hampshire: Among its many geological, mining, art and educational exhibits were a plow made by Daniel Webster and used by him on his Marshfield estate; Webster's decanter and autographed letters; and Revolutionary and Colonial relics.

New Jersey: This state exhibited in every one of the Great Buildings. Its State Building, designed to look like George Washington's headquarters at Morristown during the Revolutionary War, included reproductions of Washington's writing table, wine buffet, bedchamber and dining room.

The New Jersey Building, patterned after the house in which George Washington made his headquarters in the winter of 1779-80, was built mainly as a clubhouse for the convenience of the people of New Jersey who attended the fair.

American pride was not lacking in the Pennsylvania Building which lured big crowds with the Liberty Bell. The prized relic had been escorted under heavy security from Independence Hall to the fairgrounds.

New York: This building resembled the old Van Rensselaer residence, one of the most familiar landmarks in New York City. Huge columns of Adirondack trees supported the roof. Also displayed were statues of Christopher Columbus and Henry Hudson; a model of Fulton's steamboat; and relics from the Revolutionary War.

North Carolina: The building was constructed entirely of eighteenth-century materials brought from England. It featured an interesting collection of art and curios.

North Dakota: This state's small (3,500-square-foot) building featured one of the best school exhibits of the many shown at the fair.

Ohio: This state's original plan was to use materials donated by contractors, thus making it an exhibit of the building materials of the state. When contractors failed to show any enthusiasm, sponsors used only wood—"but in a very distinctive style."

Oregon: This young state subscribed $60,000 for its headquarters building and displays in all Great Buildings.

Pennsylvania: The building was designed to look like Independence Hall and displayed some of the most intriguing historical items shown at the fair.

The West Virginia Building was a simple structure with charming verandas.

Although it was not often mentioned in fair programs and reports, the actual Liberty Bell hung from the ceiling in this building. Also displayed were the chair in which Jefferson wrote the Declaration of Independence, the table on which it was signed and the inkwell that was used; Thomas Jefferson's sword and a lock of his hair; John Quincy Adams' baby clothes; the first portrait of George Washington; the first lightning rod invented by Benjamin Franklin; a brewing jar used by William Penn and the surveying instrument he used in laying out the city of Philadelphia; and Pocahontas' necklace.

South Carolina: This small building was designed in the style of an old French farmhouse. The state had not raised enough funds to furnish the building with appropriate displays, but sponsored elaborate agricultural, horticultural, mineral and forestry exhibits in the Great Buildings.

South Dakota: This small brick structure also was designed to look like an old French farmhouse.

Tennessee: Although this state did erect a headquarters, no description of it was recorded in official reports. It was also well represented in all Great Buildings and departments.

Texas: This 21,000-square-foot structure made of materials from the Lone Star state was built to resemble an old Spanish mission. Of the $300,000 raised in private contributions, half came from the city of Galveston.

Utah: The biggest attractions in this territory's building were a facsimile of the famous Eagle Gate to the Mormon Temple in Salt Lake City, a statue of Brigham Young and a stuffed animal exhibit that rivaled Kansas' display.

Vermont: Statuary in Vermont marble highlighted this New England state's building. It featured no products or antiquities.

Virginia: This building was nearly an exact replica, inside and out, of George Washington's Mount Vernon home, including original pictures and furniture.

Washington: Cited as one of the most interesting and largest of the state buildings at 140 feet by 220 feet, the Evergreen State built its hall entirely of timber and huge logs brought from the West Coast. It displayed the largest cedar vase ever turned from one piece of wood; a 208-foot flagstaff of red fir; a reproduction of a farm featuring a 20-foot-high wheat pyramid; a 26-ton block of coal; the largest mammoth skeleton ever found; and the largest yield of oats in the world from a single acre—156 bushels.

West Virginia: Displayed here was the sofa on which Grant and Lee sat at Appomattox while discussing terms of Lee's surrender.

Wisconsin: This building was designed in the style of many late nineteenth-century residences. A framed history of the state and logging displays were key attractions.

Wyoming: This state featured a modest French-chateau-style building with a paneled exterior decorated with hunting and pastoral scenes.

The Territories: A headquarters for territories, built in the style of a modern clubhouse, served Oklahoma, Arizona and New Mexico. The territo-

The Canada Building (at right) was a many-windowed pavilion with an inviting, open veranda. Next door is the Soda and Popcorn Pavilion, and in the background at left is the New England Clam Bake, where visitors could feast on hearty baked beans and littleneck clams.

The four largest attractions in this grouping, nestled close together across the lagoon from the Woman's Building, are (from left) Brazil's headquarters, Sweden's building, the Café de la Marine and the Fisheries Building.

ries, Alaska and the District of Columbia also exhibited throughout the Great Buildings.

Foreign Buildings

Foreign countries that exhibited at the fair did so in a variety of ways. Much like the individual states, many constructed a building and/or attraction. The many countries participating placed their most precious and impressive displays in the appropriate Great Buildings. A great many foreign buildings served more as headquarters for their officials than as exhibit halls, although some did contain exhibits. Following are highlights of the Foreign Buildings.

Austria: This country, which had postponed its International Art Jubilee from 1893 to 1894 in order to take part in the World's Columbian Exposition and to ensure that it did not draw attention away from the fair, sponsored a headquarters building on the lakeshore and elaborate displays in nearly all of the Great Buildings.

Belgium: Interestingly, this country mounted an art exhibit of greater magnitude at the World's Columbian Exposition than it had done just four years earlier closer to home at the Paris Exposition.

Brazil: In one of its courtyards, this country built a pyramid representing the forty-one tons of gold extracted from its mines between 1720 and 1810.

Canada: America's northern neighbor utilized 100,000 square feet in sponsoring both a main headquarters and provincial buildings and displays. The country made a showing in every Great Building with such key exhibits as 3,500 samples of grain, extensive minerals, the first piano ever brought into Canada and the first small hand mill for grinding grain.

Colombia: In a relatively small building (forty-five feet by forty-five feet), this country displayed a valuable collection of antiquities exhumed from prehistoric graves including water bottles, human images, helmets, trumpets, breast-plates and jewelry. It also displayed several mummies and a large collection of ancient pottery.

Costa Rica: Among its displays were a magnificent collection of tropical birds and a vast display of the barks, beans, roots, leaves, branches and pulverized woods of tropical plants used for medicinal purposes. Many visitors were amazed to see sarsaparilla plants, known to most only as a processed product in a medicine bottle or as a soda fountain drink, but which grew profusely in Costa Rica.

Cuba: Not surprisingly, Cuba was a major exhibitor in the agricultural and horticultural areas, with an especially strong showing in tobacco and cigars.

Ecuador: This little country exhibited widely in its own building as well as in the Great Buildings, featuring fascinating displays of gold and gold ore from Ibarra.

England: With 200,000 square feet of exhibit space throughout the grounds, England's total participation was greater than at any previous exposition or fair outside its own borders. England's headquarters, called the "Victoria House," was constructed of terra cotta, red brick and wood. Its interior was a picture of English comfort, with expansive fireplaces, suits of armor from the Holy War adorning the alcoves, "gossip" chairs, other antique furniture and decoration.

France: Its headquarters featured a "City of Paris," which showed forty views of the city by master French artists. France was a dominant exhibitor in numerous areas, most prominently in art and manufacturing.

Germany: This country sponsored one of the most beautiful headquarters buildings. Located on the lakefront, it had a peaked roof covered with many painted tiles, outer walls decorated in the style of old German houses with imperial eagles and allegorical figures, and huge clock towers on each corner of the building. The chimes in the towers, cast at the orders of the German emperor, were rung on German fete days during the exposition. The largest of the three bells, which weighed 7,000 pounds, required the strength of three men to ring it. Among the displays were royal jewels, relics of important historic events, artwork, a vast collection of every periodical published in Germany and rare books.

Greece: Citing severe financial problems, this country was forced to scale back its exhibits dramatically and actually required funding from the World's Columbian Exposition to create facsimile castings of major statues for display.

Guatemala: The country exhibited throughout the grounds and in its own building with more extensive displays than any other Central American country. It featured everything from a display of 5,000 orchids to hieroglyph-

The India Building, curiously enough, was designed by Chicago architect Henry Ives Cobb. Its chief exhibits revolved around tea, which visitors could sip from Indian crockery. This unique pavilion housed a magnificent collection of Indian arts and crafts valued in the hundreds of thousands of dollars.

Although Russia did not have a separate building at the fair, its exhibit within the Manufactures and Liberal Arts Building was truly stunning. The pavilion's style was unmistakably Russian and, upon entering, a visitor might feel that he was in an ancient cathedral. The finest display was of Russian furs, featuring lavish garments made of sealskin, sable, beaver, fox, mink and many other animals. One could also admire artworks in silver, bronze, glass and wood in styles quite unfamiliar to most Westerners.

ics on stones. One side of its building was devoted to manufactured products, including silks, embroideries and products made of seaweeds and water vessels made of jicara fruit and carved by craftsmen. Another of its best exhibits was a small coffee plantation demonstrating how beans are cultivated. Visitors were served steaming cups of the most fragrant coffee many had ever sampled. But perhaps its most noteworthy contribution was its talented national band, which played daily.

India: The Indian government opted not to contribute funds for displays at the exposition, but many private companies did. Several Indian princes were said to have attended the fair. The chief exhibits, in which major companies had invested several million dollars, centered around tea. Here, visitors could sip Indian tea served in beautiful hand-painted crockery by Indian servants. Other displays included Indian carpets, brass and copper utensils and antique arms inlaid with precious metals.

Italy: Following tense relations with the United States, an accord was reached in 1892 allowing the Italian government to exhibit, although it did so on a limited basis.

Japan: This was the single-largest foreign participant at the fair in terms of dollars appropriated by a foreign government. Japan erected a 40,000-square-foot building and garden complex, several buildings and attractions on the Midway and utilized some 90,000 square feet of display space in the Great Buildings. One of its most prominent contributions was the Ho-o-den, a Japanese palace, located on Wooded Island.

Mexico: With an economy far stronger than a century earlier (and later) Mexico was a major exhibitor at the fair, appropriating some $2 million.

New South Wales: This colony shared its one million square feet of space in its small headquarters and within various Great Buildings with New Zealand, Queensland and Australia. Its primary exhibits featured natural resources such as wool, minerals and wood.

Russia: Although the country was hindered by a depressed economy, it made a showing thanks to a special commission that included the "famous Count Tolstoi, the novelist and statesman."

Sandwich Islands: Hawaii was well represented throughout the fair, including its huge Hawaiian volcano diorama, one of the more earth-shattering Midway attractions.

Spain: Obviously taking a more than ordinary interest in the fair, Spain sent jewels and other possessions of Ferdinand and Isabella and many relics of Columbus.

Sweden: Its 11,000-square-foot building was constructed in Sweden, dismantled for shipment and erected again on site. It featured elaborate displays of iron products, china, glass items, gold and silver ware, wood pulp products, wax figures dressed in the charming garb of the Swedes and an outdoor sports exhibit of skates, snowshoes, sleighs, canoes and yachts.

Turkey: This country had the distinction of being the first exhibitor officially on site when a concessionaire from Constantinople raised the Turkish

This western entrance to the Midway Plaisance beckoned visitors with the Captive Balloon—a favorite amusement until it collapsed in a gale—Old Vienna on the right, and the Chinese Theatre on the left.

The Exhibits and Attractions

Twenty-four Laplanders, most from one family, traveled to Chicago with nine reindeer, a number of dogs, sleds, hunting and fishing gear and personal effects as part of the Laplander Village on the Midway. One of the attractions was a show featuring the reindeer pulling sleds around a circus ring. Although the Laplanders appeared to endure the warm Chicago climate, their reindeer did not fare as well. Despite cold baths on hot days, several of the unusual animals died during the exposition.

flag over the future location of his Midway attractions on September 20, 1891. It featured glorious mosaic floors, dazzling wall hangings, rich silks and other fabrics and weaponry.

The Midway and Private Shows

Traveling the length of the Midway Plaisance, the one-mile strip of land devoted to foreign and private exhibits, was like traveling the globe. In just a few hours, a fairgoer could pass through two Irish villages and kiss the Blarney Stone, stop for lunch in German Village, visit the bazaars of Algiers, walk through a Javanese encampment or a village of Laplanders and their reindeer, ride a donkey through a street of Cairo, view Samoans working in their grass huts or Central Africans dancing to unfamiliar rhythms, watch the thunderous eruption of Kilauea Volcano and brave a bumpy ride in a sedan chair.

This Bohemian wing of the fair—the first of its kind at a world's exposition—offered a whirlwind tour of the globe, filled with all kinds of foreign, but tantalizing sights, sounds and tastes. It was exhausting and exhilarating, and for many, it was the best part of the fair.

The exposition's general admission fee of fifty cents entitled the visitor to view all of the Great Buildings, the State and Foreign buildings, all of the grounds and even the Midway Plaisance. But many of the private shows and special events along the Midway charged an additional fee—from a dime to two dollars. Some of the attractions offered "cents off" coupons for food and goods at the pavilions, while others refunded the price of admission with a purchase.

Following is a sampling of some of the most charming, most exotic, most

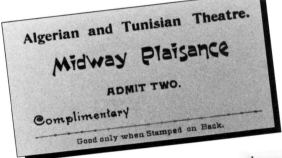

It was not the "hideous" music (a loud rattle of tambourines and shrill discordance of an Oriental lute) that attracted patrons to the Algerian Theatre, but the beautiful Arab girls who performed "languorous love dances."

Old Vienna was a quaint and picturesque reproduction of the Austrian city as it appeared in the mid-1700s, complete with cafes, shops, homes, town hall, and even the townsfolk bustling about their business. Many fairgoers lingered long hours at this Midway attraction, enjoying the scenery, the food and the omnipresent music.

compelling and most amusing attractions for visitors to the Midway Plaisance.

Algerian and Tunisian Village: Featured in this bustling village were reproductions of Tunisian and Algerian streets, sultanas from a Moorish harem, a bazaar, a cafe, a theater and more. Individual acts included snake charmers, jugglers, dancing girls and an orchestra. The dancing girls gave performances in a 1,000-seat hall. Souvenirs for sale included oriental jewelry, rugs, cushions, Arabesque tracings, perfumes and more.

Barre Sliding Railway: This water-propelled ride ran the length of the Midway.

Bernese Alps Electric Theatre: This 100-seat diorama took participants on a fifteen-minute trip to the Swiss Alps through the use of vivid scenery, sound, lights and frigid temperatures (all electrically provided). On their jour-

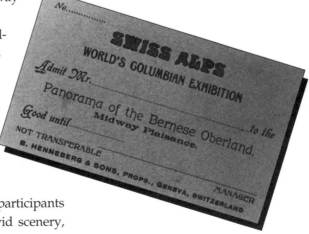

Among the attractions of "A Street in Cairo" were Egyptian swordsmen, their weapons resembling Japanese swords, rather than those more familiar to Americans and Europeans. The setting in this photograph, a temple, did not seem particularly authentic for a sword fight, but the Egyptians were convincingly dramatic.

ney visitors looked out over thirty miles of snow-covered peaks and nestling valleys in the background and a herd of cows being driven along a winding roadway by a milkmaid in the foreground. A phonograph made the experience complete, with such sounds as the tinkling of cowbells and roar of thunder.

Captive Balloon: The most expensive attraction at the fair was the tethered balloon, which took passengers aloft to a height of 1,500 feet. The balloon made two trips per hour. The fee to enter the enclosure and observe the launch was twenty-five cents; a trip aloft, which included a photograph of the passengers, was two dollars.

The balloon was a major attraction along the Midway until a powerful Chicago windstorm brought the balloon crashing to earth, terrifying passengers and the crowds of onlookers. For the latter months of the fair, a trapeze act replaced the balloon at the same location—at no charge.

July 9?

A young woman takes the stage to perform the danse du ventre or belly dance described by one writer who witnessed the controversial show: "The practice in the movement of her body rather than her feet has greatly developed [the houri dancer's] abdominal region. We are to understand that this development has increased her beauty in the Oriental imagination, as it has certainly lessened it according to Western canons of taste. The music which will accompany this performance will be of a most monotonous character, the drums, particularly, hurting the ordinary ear with their increasing sharp beats. Stamping her foot forward, the dancer will move her shoulders up and down, increasing the contortions of her body, striking the castanets she carries . . . stamping forward, each time to a posture nearer the floor, until, as she seems to expire in the excitement of the rapid music and cries of the musicians, other houris rise from their couch and take her place, or join her, waving long strips of illusion or lace in a graceful and rhythmic manner. No ordinary Western woman looked on these performances with anything but horror, and at one time it was a matter of serious debate in the councils of the Exposition whether the customs of Cairo should be faithfully reproduced, or the morals of the public faithfully protected." (The Dream City, 1893)

Chinese Village: Featured were the largest Joss House (Chinese temple) outside the great wall of China, the Chinese Theatre and cafe, acrobats, musicians and Chinese men clothed "in the raiment of the better class in Peking."

Costumed Natives: At least forty nations displayed their country's costumes. Photographs were available for twenty-five cents.

Dahomey Village: The best description of this attraction comes directly from the guidebook, *The Best Things at the World's Fair* (1893): "The natives of Dahomey, male and female, give exhibitions, consisting of war songs and dances, and showing their methods of fighting. Perched upon the gates are sentinels in full war regalia. The Amazons who fight the battles of King Behanzin, are to be seen here. They are a savage looking lot of females, masculine in appearance, and not particularly attractive. These women fought the French in recent battles. The men are small and rather effeminate in appearance."

Dutch East India Village: Two theaters, one on each side of the street, featured musical performers, jugglers and snake charmers.

Dutch Settlement: Eight South Sea Island villages were re-created and featured 300 natives in traditional garb. At the center was the Java Village, composed of twenty bamboo buildings filled with the natives' furniture, utensils, musical instruments, garments and weapons. Other villages included Sumatra, Borneo, Samoa, Fiji, New Zealand, Tonga and the Sandwich Islands. This was considered one of the most "instructive ethnological exhibitions on the Midway." Many curios were for sale.

Eiffel Tower: A twenty-five-foot model of one of the most spectacular engineering feats of the nineteenth century dazzled visitors who had not been lucky enough to view the real thing at the 1889 Paris Exposition. The tower was an exact replica to the smallest detail, from its working elevators to a miniature lighthouse atop the structure and the elaborate gardens on the

Dahomey Village showed the best of Africa, from war-whooping dances to ferocious battles.

grounds below. It was composed of 650,000 separate pieces of iron and steel (not including rivets) which, if placed end to end would form a line four miles long. At regular intervals the tower burst into a blaze of electric lights.

Ferris Wheel: By far the most visually arresting attraction on the Midway, the Ferris Wheel was also the most popular. This monster wheel, built to rival the Paris Exposition's Eiffel Tower in engineering ingenuity, carried forty people in each of its thirty-six railcar-size cabins. The colossal contrivance reached 264 feet into the air, giving riders a sweeping view of the Midway, the White City, Lake Michigan and Chicago skyline.

French Cider Press: There was no admission fee for this attraction, but people could buy a large glass of cider served by native peasant girls.

German Village: Here, at one of the largest Midway attractions, visitors could move to the lively beat of German and Bavarian bands, view a life-size village scene with Bavarian houses, the Black Forest, the Allman Tribe, town hall, a saloon, a library, marketplace, the Hessian house, Westfalia, two restaurants seating a total of 8,000, and more. The highlight of the village was a replica of a sixteenth-century castle, surrounded by a moat sixteen feet wide. Inside was "the most famous collection of weapons ever gathered in Germany . . . sixty iron dummies in full military equipment giving a complete and true picture of the weapons and armour of Germany."

Right: Samoan warriors perform one of their many character songs that fascinated Westerners. Among their performances were the "Tapate," a dance peculiar to the Wallis Islanders in which some men struck paddles together to create the beat for dancers, and many religious dances. Accompanied by a rhythmic beating of a drum, all of the songs seemed to tell detailed stories, including one called the "Mauuluulu" about the warriors' trip from their far-away island to Chicago. Another was an animated Figian cannibal dance.

Below: Admission to Java Village cost ten cents. A number of additional tickets, issued in denominations ranging from ten cents to $15, apparently could be used to purchase hand-crafted items offered in the village.

In Java Village, the largest of the South Sea Island villages that constituted the Dutch Settlement on the Midway Plaisance, visitors admired the cozy houses, bazaars, a Mohammedan church and a theater all made from natural materials such as palm leaves, grasses and split bamboo poles, the interweaving of which created a pleasing decorative effect. In the theater one could listen to the Sultan's orchestra and watch native acrobats and dancers perform. Westerners were fascinated by the glittering costumes, grotesque masks and double-jointed movements of the dancers. These same dances would be performed by beautifully dressed marionettes. Carvers, machinists, carpenters, musicians, spinners, weavers and dyers demonstrated their trades from the porches of their workshops.

Imposing as the Ferris Wheel was from a distance, towering aloft and pinpointing the fair from miles away, its internal webwork of steel was equally as impressive when viewed from one of the passenger cars.

Hagenbeck's Zoological Arena: Modeled after the Coliseum in Rome this enormous arena featured a menagerie unlike any other: bears walking tightropes, lions riding chariots, tigers harnessed to vehicles, a dwarf elephant and Miss Liebemich, the famous animal trainer guiding her ferocious actors through amazing stunts. Admission to the arena was a quarter, while performance seats varied from fifty cents to a dollar, depending upon location.

Hungarian Concert Pavilion: Gypsy bands, native performers in native dress and theatrical performances could be viewed here.

Ice Railway: Children and adults alike screamed with glee as they sped along an 850-foot-long undulating toboggan-like slide in gaily painted sleighs. Even when the Chicago sun shone brightly, the snow covering the slide stayed cold and frosty by means of two De La Vergne snow-making machines. The Ice Railway was one of the few rides at the fair designed purely for amusement.

Irish Village and Blarney Castle: The exhibit featured a community of stone cottages with thatched straw roofs and a reproduction of the celebrated ruins of Blarney Castle and the sale of native goods. Visitors who climbed the winding staircase to the top of the castle's fifty-foot tower had an excellent view of the main fairgrounds to the east. All who visited the village were presented with a piece of "genuine sod" imported from Ireland.

Japanese Bazaars: Predominantly a privately sponsored retail store, this enterprise was quickly identified as having no connection with Japan's official exhibits.

"Jim Blaine," "General Grant," "Old Abe," "Grover Cleveland," and the twenty-one other ostriches on the Midway's California Ostrich Farm delighted sightseers with their pretty plumes, gawky gaits and mischievous antics.

A taste of Irish stew and a chance to kiss the Blarney Stone were among the lures of Irish Village.

Kilauea Volcano: The largest building along the Midway, located between the Chinese Theatre and the Ferris Wheel, was the Hawaiian volcano cyclorama, said to faithfully reproduce the volcanic action of Kilauea (in a huge circular painting) in miniature.

Moorish Palace: This attraction had something for everyone: a chamber of horrors, including an execution of Marie Antoinette, a trip through Switzerland, a trip to the moon and a display of $1 million in gold coins.

Natatorium: This indoor swimming pool also featured baths and musical performances.

St. Peter's Cathedral: The model of the Roman church was constructed in one-sixteenth scale, measuring 30 feet by 45 feet and 15 feet high.

A Street in Cairo: One of the most celebrated and controversial (as well as profitable) attractions at the fair due to its scandalous belly dancers, "A Street in Cairo" offered a realistic look at how the people of Cairo lived, transacted business and amused themselves. The street was complete with mosques, temples, tombs, bazaars and other buildings capturing the general architectural flavor of Cairo. Its inhabitants were equally as authentic—Egyptian, Nubian and Sudanese men, women and children, along with their dogs, donkeys, camels and snakes. These residents gave frequent impromptu street performances, including fights, sword and candle dances, weddings and other celebrations.

Chicago Day was held October 9, 1893, to commemorate the devastation of downtown Chicago by fire twenty-two years earlier on the same day. The bird shown on the ticket is the mythological Phoenix bird, rising from the ashes and symbolizing Chicagoans' pride in overcoming the tragedy and rebuilding their downtown. Record crowds entered the fairgrounds that day.

Between the Chinese Theatre and the Ferris Wheel stood the cyclorama of the greatest active volcano in the northern hemisphere. In front of this Hawaiian exhibit on the Midway was a statue of Pele, the Hawaiian goddess of fire.

These Turks were among the several hundred professional showmen from some forty nations who lived along the Midway.

One of the many bazaars selling everything from the cheap and tawdry to tasteful and exotic in the Turkish Village.

Snake charmers and fortune tellers lined the street. But its most compelling attraction was the *danse du ventre* (belly dance). This dance, unfamiliar to most Americans—and unacceptable to many—was performed to the sounds of "Hootchy-Kootchy" music by Little Egypt and her numerous imitators.

Turkish Village: Sixty-five men, women and children from Jerusalem, Bethlehem, Nazareth, Damascus, Beirut, Lebanon, Aleppo, Constantinople and Smyrna performed a variety of plays. Also featured was a Turkish encampment consisting of mosques, kiosks and thirteen houses. Interesting displays included a 160-year-old Persian tent and a Bedouin tribe presenting all of the features of desert life: dromedaries, Arabian steeds, swords, spears and foods. In the "Wild East Show," Bedouins, outfitted with lances and swords and riding handsome steeds, portrayed the wild life of the desert nomad in mock battles. Near one of the mosques was a refreshment pavilion serving all kinds of Turkish drinks made of lemons, rose violets, bananas, tamarind raisins, licorice, oranges, pomegranates, mulberries and syrups. In a nearby cafe visitors could sample Turkish Mecca coffee and smoke Turkish tobacco in waterpipes. The 3,000-pound solid silver bed of the daughter of a Turkish sultan was a popular attraction.

Vienna Cafe and Concert Hall: Fairgoers were treated to a variety of musical entertainment and a full-service restaurant.

Venice-Murano: Visitors could watch a real glass factory in action and buy beautiful Venetian and Florentine handblown glassware and mosaics.

Of all the magnificent sights of the World's Columbian Exposition, the Court of Honor by night was one of the most spectacular. Except for a lack of spectators, this re-creation of the scene is very accurate. The moon and myriad stars pierced the sky. Tiny lights illuminated the glorious grounds and buildings. Electric searchlights flashed through the air, alternately sweeping the court and training their beams on a statue or other adornment. The water lay like a silken carpet, accented by colorful fountains.

IV

A Week at the Fair

There were many "official" guides to the fair.
Above: This sterling lapel pin of the Santa Maria was a favorite souvenir.

YOU'VE PURCHASED A GUIDEBOOK. You've studied the map. You've listened to friends' advice. You have $20 in your pocket and you're ready to spend a week at the fair. Where do you start?

There was no one "right" way to see the World's Columbian Exposition. The fair was simply too enormous and the displays too diverse for any single agenda to suit all visitors.

Most fairgoers planned their tour according to the amount of time they had to spend and personal tastes or interests. A printer might have spent an entire day in Machinery Hall, examining the most modern typesetting equipment, presses that turned out 90,000 copies per hour and folding machines that transformed flat sheets into paper accordions. An engineer might have studied those exhibits too, but he would have spent more time just gazing at the great trusses of the Manufactures and Liberal Arts Building or riding the Ferris Wheel again and again, testing and marveling at its engineering properties.

A shoemaker would have lingered in the Shoe and Leather Building, fascinated by the latest tanning processes and array of leather products. An art student would have wandered for days in the labyrinths of the Palace of Fine Arts. A farmer would have walked acre upon acre of fruit and vegetable displays, examining produce from foreign lands and then moving on to the U.S. Government Building to learn all there is to learn about combatting the pests that infest his crops.

A gardener or horticulturist would have walked in wonder among hundreds of plants that he had seen before only in books, but now were growing hardily under the glass of the Horticultural Building. A cattle breeder would have headed straight for the Stock Pavilion, wanting to return the next day and the next to compare the animals and watch the competitions.

Children would have begged for a day at the Children's Building or a ride on a gondola. Music lovers would have staged their entire trip around the scheduled performances at the bandstands and Choral Hall. Women from all countries and walks of life would have rushed to the Woman's Building to admire the works of other women. Intellectuals would have sought any number of the thousands of congresses and other educational presentations given at the World's Congress Auxiliary.

And everyone would have been drawn to the fascinations of the Midway Plaisance.

Although there was no "typical" visitor to the World's Columbian Exposition, if you were the average American couple, you traveled to Chicago from your hometown by train. You stayed at a hotel in the city or with relatives nearby. You had limited funds and just seven days to spend at this once-in-a-lifetime extravaganza. Your adventure might have unfolded as follows.

One of the most crowded spots at the fair was early morning outside the Terminal Station, where a daily tide of some 100,000 arrived by train—and literally rushed to the beckoning sights. "Many among this throng are daily and persistent visitors; others are out from the city for their periodical 'day off,' but it may safely be inferred that the majority of this eager, hurrying crowd is made up of country-folk and other persons from a distance to whom this one bright day may be the event of a toilsome life." (The Columbian Gallery, 1894)

Many sightseers ventured to the fairgrounds from Chicago on one of several steamships plying the waters of Lake Michigan.

A four-oared, swan-beaked gondola glides through the South Canal in front of the Agricultural Building.

The First Day

There were many ways to get to the fair. You could take a picturesque steamer ride from downtown Chicago to the Casino Pier. You could board the Illinois Central Railroad or the elevated railway, which took you directly onto and throughout the grounds. You could ride a cable car, hike the six miles from town (most unlikely!) or hire a taxi (most expensive!).

For your first day's approach you chose the steamship. Your plan was to spend most of the day around the Grand Basin, touring the grounds, getting your bearings and drinking in the external beauty of the buildings—a perfect way to sample the vastness and excitement of the fair.

Landing at the Casino Pier, you left the steamer and immediately boarded the Movable Sidewalk which transported you to shore. You purchased your fifty-cent general admission ticket and passed through the turnstiles adjacent to the Casino. You headed directly for the Peristyle, the immense colonnade representing the forty-eight states and territories. You located your state's column, craning your neck to see the architect's rendition of your coat-of-arms and the statue above it.

Passing through the center of this grand entrance you stopped short, transfixed by one of the most magnificent views of the fair: The Court of Honor. The buildings were almost blinding in their whiteness, yet dreamlike in their reflections on the emerald-tinted waters of the Grand Basin. You gazed with pride at the lofty *Statue of the Republic* rising from the east end of the basin. Opposite, you saw the stately *MacMonnies Fountain*, its jets of water glistening in the sun, and beyond, the gilded dome of the Administration Building, sparkling like a gem in the center of a brooch.

You turned left, choosing to begin your tour on the southern side of the court. There, you confronted the noble Agricultural Building, its massive dome topped by Saint-Gaudens' famous *Statue of Diana*. Next, as you neared Machinery Hall you heard the whirs and clanks of machines on display. As you

rounded the western end of the Grand Basin you admired the fountains and gardens adorning the expansive court of the Administration Building.

You avoided the railroad terminal, where swarms of people were arriving at the fair, moving instead toward the Electricity, Mines and Mining, and Transportation buildings. You paused to admire the Transportation Building's "Golden Doorway," but were soon drawn to the imposing panorama of canals, bridges, walkways, shrubbery and flowers stretching for a half-mile in front of you. Here, you chose to take the westerly route around the Main Lagoon, crossing a Rialto bridge onto Wooded Island and strolling through the picturesque rose garden. You stopped for a cup of Oriental tea and relaxed near the Japanese Ho-o-den to reflect on all you had seen so far.

Eager to move on, you passed Choral Hall, where you checked the schedule for performances later in the week. Sweet scents greeted you as you passed the Horticultural Building. Directly across the lagoon you saw another imposing dome, this one atop the U.S. Government Building. Beyond was the intriguing Fisheries Building.

Next you passed the Woman's Building and the entrance to the Mid-

Above: Taken from Chicago's Tower Hotel, this panoramic view of the exposition and nearby city buildings shows the efficient system of rail lines connecting with the Terminal Station. Several key buildings can be identified by their domes (from left): Illinois, Horticultural, Fisheries, U.S. Government and Administration. The Manufactures and Liberal Arts Building is to the left of the Administration Building.

way. Though the brilliant colors and pulsating sounds drifting from the Midway were tempting, you stuck to your plan.

You had seen many concessions along your half-day journey: those for food, drink and souvenirs. But you planned to have lunch at the New England Clam Bake, and the souvenirs could wait until you'd sampled the interiors of your favorite buildings.

As you reached the northern portion of the grounds you saw the huge Palace of Fine Arts and the Illinois Building, but you were more interested in locating *your* state building—even taking a quick look inside.

You also took time for a short tour of the Eskimo Village, with only a handful of its sixty "real-life" Eskimos left after the rest rebelled. You admired their walrus-skin houses, Husky dogs and harpoons before you ventured into the area of the foreign headquarters buildings. Indeed, you felt like a foreigner transplanted into a bustling village of unfamiliar architecture, decoration and languages.

After a hearty meal of littleneck clams and baked beans at the Clam Bake you walked a short distance to the Naval Exhibit. You boarded the in-

Strolling down this avenue of the State Buildings was like wandering through America in miniature.

credible replica of the warship *Illinois*, amazed to find that it was not the "real" thing, but was actually built on pilings.

Cooled by the brisk breeze blowing off Lake Michigan, you proceeded down the narrow strip of land alongside the Manufactures and Liberal Arts Building. There, you encountered jolly musical bands and other performers. You stopped for a delicious chocolate treat at Walter Baker & Company's concession and then passed by the Music Hall to arrive back at the Peristyle.

You continued south, rounding the Agricultural Building and taking a quick glance at the exteriors of the Krupp Gun House, Shoe and Leather Building, Forestry Building, Stock Pavilion, sawmill and cattle sheds.

You ended your tour in the waning daylight at the Monastery of La Rabida, where you couldn't resist going inside to view the invaluable collection of Columbus relics—a fitting finale to your first day at the World's Columbian Exposition.

The Rest of the Week

By the second day you were ready for some intensive exhibit viewing. Traveling by train to the grounds, you arrived at the Terminal Station at the western end of the Court of Honor. The magnificence of it all again took your breath away, and you were tempted to tour the grounds once again; but your mission was to spend the entire day in the Manufactures and Liberal Arts Building.

Like an infant overstimulated by too many sounds, sights or touches, you had reached sensory overload after just three hours in the great hall. You took time for some fresh air and lunch, this time a several-course meal at a French cafe. Then it was back to the Manufactures for another dose of amazement upon amazement in the entrancing displays of all the things that man had built.

A colony of Esquimaux (Eskimos) from the far north region of Labrador, arrived in Chicago a full six months before the fair opened to acclimatize themselves to the warm weather. They were admitted to Jackson Park where they built a stockade and charged an admission fee. But when summer struck, ten of the twelve tribes threw aside their fur coats and quit the exposition, claiming that they had been deceived by the contractor who had taken them from home. This photo shows the nearly deserted settlement with some of the remaining tribesmen playing with "black snake" whips. A typically small crowd of spectators looked on. One reporter commented, "Had the Esquimaux settled on Midway Plaisance and held together, their remarkable ethnological character would have received earnest public attention."

In the late afternoon you took a short stroll to see Columbus' caravels, climbing aboard the *Santa Maria* and wondering how the voyager and his crew could have persevered or even survived in such a small vessel. After a leisurely dinner of homestyle "American" food (boiled meat and potatoes) at the massive Casino Restaurant, you headed for a prized bench seat near the Grand Basin to view the magical "light fantastic."

Darkness fell and you watched in wonder as the electrical fountains tossed up masses of illuminated water in a rainbow of colors. Then lights appeared on every rooftop and throughout the grounds and waterways creating a twinkling fairyland—a spectacle almost unbelievable to most people in the nineteenth century. Three huge spotlights, installed at the top of the Manufactures and Liberal Arts and other buildings, swept over the grounds, resting momentarily on fountains and statues, such as the *Diana*. While it was barely touted as such at the time, the World's Columbian Exposition was the first fair ever to be so illuminated and to take advantage of Thomas Edison's marvelous incandescent lights.

The next morning you tackled four Great Buildings: Machinery Hall, Mines and Mining, Electricity and Transportation. Realizing that ideally one would spend at least a day in each building, you paced yourself carefully.

The displays in each of these buildings complemented those in the Manufactures and Liberal Arts Building and you began to grasp a more complete picture of the historical connections of man and machinery. In the Electricity Building alone you toured ten acres of dynamos, batteries, heaters, telephones, motors, lights and other devices of which your parents knew nothing and which had become everyday conveniences for your generation.

A highlight of the morning was an elevator ride up to the 165-foot-high cupola of the Transportation Building for a panoramic view of the fairgrounds and surrounding country.

In the late afternoon, seeking relief from your exhilarating, but deafening tour of mechanical contrivances, you boarded a gondola for a peaceful tour of the waterways. Here, you reflected on the mastery of Olmsted's plan. The layout was remarkable in its contradiction: The grounds were overflowing with exhibits that bombarded the mind with the excitement of human progress, but were interwoven with serene waterways that simply insisted a visitor slow down, relax and observe it all at a snail's pace.

You ended the day by attending a performance at Choral Hall, followed by a forty-minute, ten-cent ride around the grounds on the elevated railway.

On the fourth day you reveled in the relationship between man and nature. First, you toured the Agricultural Building, one of the most beautiful structures on the grounds. Eighteen acres of nature's bounty beckoned you: green fields and pastures, cereals, grasses and forage plants, sugars and confections, dairy products and foods—all that was suggestive of harvests from the earth.

You also toured the livestock exhibits, spending two or three hours eyeing the horses, cattle, sheep, camels, goats, swine, dogs, cats, ferrets, rabbits and assorted wild animals, and watching the best of the bunch perform in the arena.

Desiring a more fragrant ending to the day, you proceeded to the Horticultural Building and its soothing flowers, palms, grottoes and fountains.

You allocated the morning of the fifth day to the Woman's and Children's buildings and the Palace of Fine Arts. Though you could easily have spent a day in each, you had to move at a swift clip to ensure you at least saw the finest exhibits in each. You wisely devoted the bulk of your time to the Fine Arts where hours passed like minutes as you studied the masterpieces of the world's greatest painters, sculptors, etchers, carvers and other artists.

Our Journey

On the 11th of September 1893, father, mother, Rob Strong and I left home about seven oclock A.M. We took the cars at New Milford for Danbury, and after three hours waiting, we at last started for Chicago, about three oclock P.M.

September 13th we arrived at Chicago and met Uncle Ralph, and after getting our breakfast, we started for the fair.

The "White City," beautiful by day, was almost like fairy land in the evening. The dome of the Administration building was beautifully illuminated by electric lights, looking as much like candles as anything. . . . Very powerful search lights, said to be the largest ever used, were thrown from the top of the Manufactures building. It would fall on a piece of statuary, or the front of a building, and bring out every bit of it, even plainer than in the brightest sunshine. Sometimes the light was red or green, and then the
statuary look red, or green, but was not as pretty as the white. . . .

The fire-works were beautiful too. Some-times they were on the lake-front and sometimes on the lagoon. We were there Ohio day and there was a fine display. There would be a dozen or more rockets sent up at once, and they would all explode together, almost filling the air with red, blue and green stars, which floated in the air for a moment, and then dropped slowly into the water.

—Unknown fairgoer's diary

The preceding entry was excerpted from a 54-page, handwritten diary of a summer vacation. Bound with faded blue ribbons and etched hardbound cover titled "Vacation Days," the diary appears to have been written by a young teenager, based on references, tone and language. The diary is part of the World's Columbian Exposition Collection at the Chicago Public Library, Special Collections Department.

Though fairgoers often took a break from exhibit viewing and simply rested along the shores of seductive Lake Michigan, these visitors appear to have congregated for one of the many boat shows presented on special fete days.

Early afternoon was reserved for the Fisheries Building, which, with its elaborate aquariums and sparkling ponds offered a refreshing respite from the Chicago heat. Though not a fisherman, you were captivated by the brilliant colors of the myriad sealife. You then moved on to the U.S. Government Building and its surprisingly clever displays from nearly every governmental department.

By the sixth day, like most visitors, you needed a reprieve from the intensity and intellectual stimulation of the fair. You were ready for the Midway!

Entry to this first-of-its-kind amusement area of the fair was free, but many of the concessions were "calculated to draw a visitor's last nickel," according to one reporter. Fair officials even admitted their hopes that the Midway would help ensure the financial success of the fair.

You were as eager as any to sample this magical mile. One of your first thrills was the Barre Sliding Railway, a water-propelled ride that whisked you from one end of the Midway to the other at the dizzying speed of 100 miles per hour.

Making your way west along the strip you encountered the Libbey Glass concession, where you watched craftsmen blow beautiful glass vases and bought a stunning spun-glass tie. (The Infanta of Spain, one of the many dignitaries attending the fair, had also stopped by the Libbey concession and was so impressed with a spun-glass dress on display that she ordered one to take home).

Trinkets and Treasures for All

In the 1990s many of us feel inundated by opportunities to buy souvenirs. Hawkers hound us, and our children nag us at every fair and festival, picnic and parade—even at the corner gas station. Although we may think this preoccupation with mementos is a modern-day phenomenon, in fact it was very much an obsession with fairgoers one hundred years ago.

The World's Columbian Exposition offered numerous souvenirs to fit the taste and pocketbook of every fairgoer. The collecting spree started at the entrance gate with the beautiful, engraved fifty-cent general admission ticket. Issued in a colorful set of six, the tickets featured the likenesses of Christopher Columbus, Benjamin Franklin, George Handel, Abraham Lincoln, George Washington and an American Indian. There were also dozens of special day or individual attraction tickets and passes that fairgoers hoarded to paste in treasured scrapbooks.

Columbus was, of course, a popular souvenir subject, featured in a variety of poses on a variety of objects. One of the most famous was the first-ever United States commemorative coin, the half dollar minted in both 1892 and 1893 to raise funds for the fair. The fair's namesake was also featured on everything from glassware and silk scarves to stick pins and photo albums.

The first U.S. coin bearing a portrait of a woman was minted for the fair. The Isabella quarter, issued to mark the aid given by Queen Isabella of Spain to Columbus, remains today as the only U.S. commemorative quarter ever struck. Forty thousand of the quarters were minted, making them rare numismatic collectors' items.

The exposition spawned hundreds of other coins, tokens and medals, many of them minted in the new metal of the era—aluminum. Some of the more expensive pieces were ornate, while others were little more than simple trade tokens.

The official award medal for winners of display competitions in the Great Buildings was also available as a souvenir. The beautiful medal was designed by Augustus Saint-Gaudens, designer of the *Statue of Diana* atop the Agricultural Building, and Charles Barber, well-

This metal box, approximately two inches by four inches, is one of many tin, pewter and wooden container souvenirs spawned by the fair.

Above: The official exhibitor's award medal is a prized collectible today. Right: The hanging and pin back badges created for special days and events, such as Columbus Day, were popular souvenirs.

Many souvenirs, such as these playing cards, highlighted the architecture of the exposition.

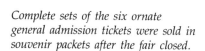

known for his U.S. coinage designs. Columbian stamps and miniature admission tickets were also available encased in aluminum medals.

Next to Columbus, the most popular subject featured in souvenirs was the architecture of the exposition. The Court of Honor and individual buildings were depicted on everything from plates and pincushions to postcards and playing cards. Some of the most elegant depictions were found in beautiful lithographs by several American and European companies and colorful paperweights by Libbey Glass.

The Ferris Wheel was another favorite item. It adorned medals and brooches, matchboxes and calling cards. It was also shown in three-dimensional images viewed through stereopticons.

The list of official fair collectibles was long and varied, to say the least. Items ranged from the cheap and tawdry to the tasteful and elegant. Popular among women visitors were miniature mother-of-pearl purses decorated with likenesses of Columbus and scenes of the fair. There were also hand-painted scarves, delicate jewelry and colorful cloth fans. For the more practical fairgoer there were bamboo placemats and ceramic pitchers.

Men gravitated toward the matchsafes, razors and cigar cutters engraved with exposition highlights. For children there were pencil boxes, dominoes, a silver puzzle in the shape of an egg, and even a toy cigar that opened into a colored banner of the fair.

Among the most valuable relics of the exposition today are several coin banks. One mechanical bank features Columbus sitting on a tree stump. When a coin is inserted, a mound of dirt pops up and an Indian greets Columbus. Another bank is a silver-plated replica of the Administration Building.

Many souvenirs were made onsite. Thomas Stevens of London hand wove silk pictures and ribbons on his portable loom in Machinery Hall. These pictures, known today as Stevengraphs, are some of the most valuable collectors' items from the fair. Many other silk items, such as woven bookmarks and ribbons, were made or decorated on the spot.

Numerous souvenirs were made simply to advertise exhibitors' wares. Packets of sewing needles, boxes of complexion soaps, silk samples, trade cards and fancy stationery all sported their sponsor's name, a reference to the fair and a bit of advertising copy.

Not always included on the official list of souvenirs, the Midway generated an array of mementos. It had its share of flimsy and phoney trinkets proffered by enterprising foreigners, but there were also many authentic and original items. Some of the offerings, like the "genuine piece of sod from Ireland," were free; others, such as Persian and Turkish rugs, were pricey.

Fortunately for collectors and historians, as well as descendants of those who attended the fair, many souvenirs from the World's Columbian Exposition still exist today. These mementos, whether treasured for monetary value or sentimental reasons, offer a tangible glimpse of the most glorious of world's fairs.

Complete sets of the six ornate general admission tickets were sold in souvenir packets after the fair closed.

Many souvenir ribbons were woven at the fair.

Hagenbeck's Arena on the Midway featured an assortment of wild animals performing unbelievable feats.

You also took in a performance of the Hagenbeck troupe of animal entertainers: bears doing the "William Tell" act, lions driving chariots, camels roller skating, parrots supposedly talking to one another in sixty-five different languages and a hippopotamus swinging on a trapeze (of sorts).

Still shaking your head at the wonders of the trained-animal world, you walked just a few yards to the villages of the South Sea Islanders. Here you splurged on a beautiful shirt made of pineapple fibers and viewed the strange Javanese village with its "wild man of Borneo" locked in a cage, a collection of bamboo huts and furniture made of tiger and rhinoceros skins.

Braving the scorn of Victorian women, you eagerly marched down "A Street in Cairo," amidst its authentic wedding procession, camels, donkeys, three hundred Arabs, snake charmers (who swore by Allah that the exaggerated garter snakes they used were the most deadly of all serpents) and sword-swallowers to attend one of the most controversial attractions at the fair, the "dans du ventre," or belly dance. Fully satisfied that you had seen the real "Little Egypt" and that her dance was as exotic though perhaps not as erotic as expected, you headed for the technological marvel of the Midway.

A ride on the Ferris Wheel was perhaps the most thrilling of the fair—as was the view when you stopped at the top. Being carried 264 feet skyward in a cubicle on a revolving wheel was one of the most novel and thrilling sensations you'd ever experienced.

Back on solid ground, you proceeded to the Algerian and Tunisian villages where you saw "a host of savage, swarthy, but picturesque people of Tunis and Algiers dance and play music, cook and serve food . . . some native Arab fanatics among them, eating scorpions, cutting and piercing themselves with evil-looking weapons, and generally behaving so as to be interesting but totally unsuited to attend a family tea party," according to one fairgoer.

You risked a lunch at the Moorish Cafe, a reproduction of a north African inn serving the blackest coffee you'd ever seen and dishes "of questionable composition." A string band "playing monotonous repetitions,"

Many visitors said goodbye to the fair with a last dash through the Midway and a leisurely stroll back past the Woman's Building to the pier or train station.

entertained you with music quite foreign and not particularly soothing to your ears.

After a quick look at an exploding volcano, an Austrian Village, a Chinese temple and screaming Dahomeyan warriors, you called it a day—one of the best days you'd spent at the fair.

The Last Day

You approached your last day at the exposition with both relief and regret. It had been a long, exhausting week, but today was your last chance to commit to memory the many exhibits and attractions most important to you, to savor it before it vanished like a brilliant rainbow. Certainly, one part of you was so overwhelmed with the excitement and assault on all your senses that you were ready to leave the fair. But another part hungered for more and sought desperately to drink in as much as possible before it all ended forever.

You retraced your steps through parts of your favorite buildings, wandered even a bit aimlessly through the grounds to see some of the smaller buildings you hadn't had time for earlier. You took a leisurely ride on a motor launch and gazed at the magnificent White City. In the late afternoon you turned once again for the Midway. It would be easy to spend your last two dollars; it would be easy to stay here long into the evening.

You collected a few postcards, bought a couple of buttons and ribbons to tuck away at home, and couldn't resist buying just one more gift—a little ruby glass toothpick holder for a friend. Some dark winter evening in the coming century you'd retrieve your trinkets from a dresser drawer and rekindle happy memories of the fair to end all fairs. And oh, how your grandchildren would love the stories that went with them.

Epilogue

DURING OCTOBER 1893, THE LAST MONTH of the fair, attendance swelled to record numbers. On Chicago Day, October 9, more than three quarters of a million people passed through the turnstiles.

Equally huge crowds were anticipated for the elaborate ceremonies planned for closing day. But three days before the celebration, Chicago's popular Mayor Carter Harrison was assassinated by a disgruntled office seeker, and a darkness fell over the city. The fair closed quietly, with its flags at half-mast, its visitors somber and its orchestra playing Beethoven's *Funeral March*.

The process of dismantling the White City, formally and informally, began immediately. Guards were posted to keep thieves and vandals away. Governments and private exhibitors removed crates and shipping materials from a huge storage facility near the rail terminals at the southern end of the grounds and began the arduous task of packing and shipping the invaluable materials displayed at the fair.

A year later most of the White City's gleaming buildings were gone. First to disappear were the Casino, Music Hall, Peristyle and Movable Sidewalk, all destroyed by fire in January 1894. Several months later the buildings of the Court of Honor had also burned to the ground in a series of spectacular and accidental blazes. Most of the other Great Buildings were razed for scrap metal.

Some of the State, Foreign and Auxiliary buildings were sold intact to be relocated to other sites and used as homes, galleries, offices or for other purposes. Among them were the Connecticut, Ceylon, Delaware, South Dakota, New Jersey, Pennsylvania, Rhode Island, Idaho, Wisconsin and Victoria buildings. Though many of them survived for several decades, ultimately all

The Cold Storage Building, housing an ice skating rink and the fair's ice-making facility, burned in a tragic fire on July 10, 1893. As horrified fairgoers watched, thirteen firemen and four workers trapped by the flames fell to their deaths from the building's tower.

were lost to fire, disrepair or the wrecker's ball. The Victoria and Wisconsin buildings lasted the longest; they both had ended up in Kansas City, where Daniel Burns Dyer, a prominent businessman, combined them with several buildings he had obtained from the 1904 St. Louis World's Fair to build a huge private estate. Dyer died in 1912, and after several changes of ownership, the mammoth complex was torn down in 1940.

A few buildings remained on the grounds, until they, too, burned or were demolished for scrap. The German Building served as a restaurant until 1925 when it was destroyed by fire. The Iowa Building remained on the site until it was torn down in 1936. The Ho-o-den, originally donated by the Japanese government and intended to remain as a permanent structure, was destroyed by fire in the 1940s.

Only four of the original buildings from the World's Columbian Exposition still stand today. The Palace of Fine Arts—the lone surviving Great Building—is the only original building remaining on the fairgrounds. Located on North Pond, it is now Chicago's Museum of Science and Industry.

Another survivor is the Maine Building, which was purchased immediately after the fair closed by Hiram Rickers and Sons, winners of an exposition award medal for their Poland Spring Water. The Rickers moved the building aboard a sixteen-car train from Chicago to their world-famous Maine resort where it became an art gallery and library. It changed hands several times and pieces of its interior were sold, but the building still stands in Poland Spring today. It is listed on the National Register of Historic Places and is open to the public during the summer.

Another surviving structure is the Dutch House, which was used by Van Houten & Zoon Cocoa Company during the exposition. It stands today in Brookline, Massachusetts, where it is a popular tourist attraction.

The last of the four remaining buildings is the Norway Building, which was moved from the fair to the William Wrigley estate at Lake Geneva, Wisconsin, and later to Blue Mounds, Wisconsin, where it attracts thousands of visitors each year.

The Midway Plaisance, once the rowdy and bustling promenade of exotic exhibits, today is a dignified drive on the University of Chicago campus.

The Fate of the Wheel

The jewel of the Midway in 1893, George Ferris' amazing wheel, suffered a fate similar to that of most of the buildings. After the exposition closed, the wheel was allowed to continue turning for a few more days to accommodate the demand of additional passengers. It remained on the grounds for several months while crews dismantled it, and George Ferris, embroiled in a dispute with exposition officials over the $100,000 in profits generated by his invention, sought an interested buyer or fair sponsor. In the meantime, Chicago police arrested three men attempting to steal a wagon full of Ferris Wheel parts.

Ferris moved the wheel to another site in Chicago, but it attracted more complaints from neighbors than paying customers. Over the next decade the wheel was relocated several times, but it never achieved a modicum of the success it enjoyed as the centerpiece of the World's Columbian Exposition. Unfortunately, neither did George Ferris, who died suddenly in 1896 at the age of 37. After the wheel's last appearance at the St. Louis World's Fair in 1904, "the wonder of two continents" was dynamited and sold for scrap—but not before it spawned the contemporary versions that we have come to know today.

A Far-Reaching Legacy

Once the buildings are gone and the displays are returned to their inventors, manufacturers, governments, museums or archives, often all that remains of a world's fair are the memories of its visitors and its assortment of souvenirs.

Fittingly, the most glorious of world's fairs left an abundance of souvenirs. Thousands of objects are held in museums or private collections. Hundreds of books, periodicals and pamphlets detailing the fair can be found in libraries and collector's hands. (Even Mark Twain journeyed to Chicago with plans to see the White City. In typical Twain fashion, he never reached the grounds, but published a lengthy piece on his misadventures in Chicago.)

The fair was well-documented in photography. The works of innumerable photographers, including official photographer Charles Dudley Arnold, fill the pages of this book. Arnold was hired to document the fair from construction through closing, and several archives today are bursting with his images. Other professionals did the same for sponsors, publishers and agencies. The only areas lacking in photographic coverage, at least in comparison to the vast selection of images of the buildings and grounds, are interior photographs and action images, both difficult to shoot due to film and shutter speed limitations a century ago.

But more than the physical souvenirs and documentation, the World's Columbian Exposition left a far-reaching legacy of architectural, scientific and cultural impact.

Women's involvement in the fair greatly advanced the cause of women's suffrage and other issues. The extensive participation by foreign nations helped promote international cooperation and understanding at government, as well as grass-roots levels. Reportedly, numerous international business deals were struck by exhibitors impressed by each other's wares and potential for expansion.

Many scientific advancements and applications to industry can be traced to the exposition—both those that were inspired by the opportunity to exhibit and those that were created after viewing a competitor's genius. The installation in Chicago of the first electric transit system in the United States and the use of electric lighting for purely decorative purposes were direct results of the fair.

The Maine Building is the only State Building still standing today. It is a popular tourist attraction in Poland Spring, Maine, and is listed on the National Register of Historic Places.

Never before had so many experts in so many different fields congregated at a single location. Nearly 6,000 addresses were presented before 700,000 people as part of the World's Congress Auxiliary, which was held in conjunction with the fair. The congress, featuring a series of meetings and symposia on almost every scholarly and cultural topic affecting the rapidly changing society of the 1890s, was organized as a permanent tribute to the principles of the exposition—to promote understanding, intelligence and industry. As such, it provided fertile ground for new ideas.

In the cultural arena, Anton Dvorak composed his *New World Symphony* for a production that was to be enacted in a 12,000-seat "Spectatorium," with

The Security Department's Report

Every department of the World's Columbian Exposition kept copious notes during the fair. The final report compiled by the director of works alone filled eight book-length volumes, and those by other directors, managers and superintendents were nearly as cumbersome. Each participating state published a lengthy report—in some cases, even a hard-cover book—detailing its finances, successes and failures.

The Security Department's report contained an odd collection of both humorous and tragic statistics on the fair:

- Persons taken into custody for petty pilfering and put off grounds on paying for goods taken 421
- Arrests 954
- Convictions 438
- Acquittals 94
- Escapes 1
- Number of reports on children lost 30
- Number of reports on children restored to parents 20
- Number of reports of shadowy, suspicious persons 539
- Number of reports of persons getting over fence into grounds 408
- Number of reports of Zulu acting improperly 1
- Number of reports of finding fetus on grounds 3
- Number of reports of employees killed 5
- Number of reports of ex-convicts on grounds 135

The Columbian Guard was a complement of 2,000 police, fire and guard staff hired and managed by the exposition. Though they "lacked the city policeman's bulk and experience," they were the "best obtainable." Candidates were subjected to an exhaustive physical examination before being accepted. They had to be at least five feet eight inches in height and between twenty-one and twenty-five years of age, and "were required to furnish testimonials as to former good character and habits."

- Number of reports of patrol wagons colliding with ambulance 2
- Number of reports of attempts to gain admission with fraudulent passes 33
- Number of reports of Kodaks without permit 30
- Number of reports of taking photographs without permit 37
- Number of reports of attempt to pass counterfeit coin 10

twenty-five moving stages, planned for the exposition. Unfortunately, the sponsor ran out of money after spending $500,000, the building was never finished and the symphony was never heard—at least not at the fair.

Poet Katherine Lee Bates was said to have been so moved by the image of the fair that she wrote *America the Beautiful*. L. Frank Baum was said to have found inspiration for his famous Emerald City in his tours of the White City.

More than any other aspect, the architecture of the World's Columbian Exposition had the greatest visible impact on America. Well into the next century, critics volleyed opinions on the overall design of the fair, alternately praising its innovation and cohesiveness at one extreme and lambasting its reliance on the old schools at the other. Today, both opinions are considered exaggerated.

But it remains undisputed that the fair provided an extraordinary stimulus to interprofessional arts. Daniel Burnham's vision in bringing together the best minds in all disciplines of design and promoting a collaborative spirit was seen as the means to excellence in architecture.

The alabaster city awakened an unprecedented public interest in civic planning and design. Americans became fascinated with the possibility of transforming the dreary urban environment of their hometowns with Burnham's "City Beautiful" plan. Frequently working with Frederick Olmsted and several of the architects of the Great Buildings, Burnham was hired to incorporate his plan in cities such as Chicago, Cleveland, Washington, D.C., and San Francisco. Today, the best parts of many American cities are still spacious, with wide boulevards and decorative landscaping, thanks to Burnham's influence.

As with most world's fairs, the goals of the World's Columbian Exposition were to educate, celebrate and entertain. By all measures, it more than succeeded. Stockholders left with a small profit; nations returned home with greater understanding of their foreign neighbors, and individuals left with new insight into the state of mankind.

But the legacy of the fair ran deeper. By tracing so magnificently the progress of 400 years, the World's Columbian Exposition infused America with new hope and spirit as it entered the twentieth century—and a new age of discovery.

"To him who has taken part in a battle nothing has a charm quite equal to revisiting it.

"The World's Fair was not unlike a battle to the men who designed and operated it, and, were the buildings still standing, it would be easy to thrill your hearts with the stories of things that happened where you might be standing. But all signs of the exposition have passed away.

"I never expect to meet again men whose minds glowed with brilliant thought, but more than that, men who were great enough to realize that everyone comes to his very best when cooperating with others, and that the success of the whole is the thing of importance."

—Daniel Burnham, excerpt of penciled draft of speech

Acknowledgments

IN RESEARCHING AND WRITING THIS BOOK we contacted numerous archives and other sources specializing in Columbiana and the World's Columbian Exposition. Among the sources, two archives and two archivists stand out as key contributors to the book. We are deeply grateful to archivist Andrea Mark at the Special Collections Department of the Chicago Public Library for her help with our initial onsite research, her willingness at every stage of the writing to answer questions at a moment's notice (which often meant digging into the archives) and her unflagging enthusiasm and encouragement. Mark's colleague, Galen Wilson, was extremely helpful in providing photographs, primary research material and ephemera from the library.

We are equally grateful to archivist Mary Woolever, who helped us wade through the wonderfully informative archives at the Art Institute of Chicago. Her guidance on architectural descriptions of the fair and her painstaking review of the final manuscript (including hours-long phone conversations) were invaluable in ensuring the integrity of the book.

We would also like to thank the numerous collectors and dealers, including Tom Diddle, Chuck Kirtley and Tony Swicer, who helped us locate and identify many of the souvenirs and ephemera used in the book.

We are indebted to Jim Emple, a journalist in Bangor, Maine, for sharing his extensive research for the epilogue.

As always, we thank the staff of Laing Communications for their enormous contributions to the project: Sandra Harner, art director, for her dedication, attention to detail and patience with our frenzy; Anita Hardy, for help with indexing, proofreading and editorial assistance; Nancy Estle, for last-minute editorial research and production; and Mary Laing, for photo logging and general assistance.

Finally, special thanks to Roberta Patterson, for handling many other details of our lives with her usual devotion while we were consumed by the book.

Selected Bibliography

Anderson, Norman D., and Walter R. Brown. *Ferris Wheels*. New York: Random House, 1983.

Appelbaum, Stanley. *The Chicago World's Fair of 1893*. New York: Dover Publications, Inc., 1980.

Arnold, C. D., and H. D. Higinbotham. *Official Views of the World's Columbian Exposition*. Chicago: Chicago Photo-Gravure Co., 1893.

The Art Institute of Chicago. D. H. Burnham Collection. Draft of a speech by Burnham, Chief of Construction and Director of Works for the World's Columbian Exposition.

Badger, Reid. *The Great American Fair*. Chicago: Nelson-Hall, 1979.

Bancroft, Hubert Howe. *The Book of the Fair. An Historical and Descriptive Presentation of the World's Science, Art, and Industry, As Viewed through the Columbian Exposition at Chicago in 1893*. Vol. 1. New York: Bounty Books, 1894.

Blaine, James G., J. W. Buel, John Clark Ridpath, and Benjamin Butterworth. *Columbus and Columbiana: A Pictorial History of the Man and the Nation*. New York: Hunt & Eaton, 1892.

Blaske, Mary Steffek. "World's Columbian Exposition. Eating Your Way Down Memory Lane." *World's Fair* 2, no. 3 (Summer 1982).

California World's Fair Commission. *Final Report: California at the World's Columbian Exposition*. Sacramento: Sacramento State Office, A. J. Johnston, Superintendent of Printing, 1894.

Cameron, William E. *World's Columbian Exposition 1893. The World's Fair, being a Pictorial History of the Columbian Exposition*. Philadelphia: The Thompson Publishing Co., 1893.

Chicago and Her Two World's Fairs. N.p.: Geographical Publishing, 1933.

Chicago and the World's Fair. New York and Chicago: A. Witteman, The Albertype Co., 1893.

Chicago Public Library, Special Collections Department, World's Columbian Exposition Collection. Final Report of the Director of Works. Excerpt from final statistical reports of security forces [1894].

_____. Hand-written diary of a teenager, "Vacation Days." Excerpt dated September 1893.

The City of Palaces. Picturesque World's Fair. Chicago: W. B. Conkey Co., 1894.

The Columbian Gallery of World's Fair Views: A Portfolio of Photographs from the World's Fair. Chicago: The Werner Co., 1894.

Columbian Gallery: A Portfolio of Photographs of the World's Fair. Chicago: The Werner Co., 1894.

Cottrell, Beekman W. "The Pride of America: George Ferris's Wonderful Wheel." *World's Fair* 1, no. 3 (Summer 1981): 1-5.

Doolin, James P. *1893—Columbian Exposition, Admission and Concession Tickets*. Dallas: Doolco Inc., 1981.

The Dream City, A Portfolio of Photographic Views of the World's Columbian Exposition. Introduction by Prof. Halsey C. Ives, Chief of the Department of Fine Arts. St. Louis: N.D. Thompson Publishing Co., 1893.

1893 World's Columbian Exposition. N.p.: B.F. Larrabee & Co., n.d.

Evans, Elwood, and Edmond S. Meany, eds. *The State of Washington: A Brief History of the Discovery, Settlement and Organization of Washington.* Tacoma: State of Washington World's Fair Commission, 1893.

Fame's Tribute to Children. Being a Collection of Autograph Sentiments Contributed by Famous Men & Women for This Volume. Done in Fac-simile [sic] and Published for the Benefit of the Children's Home, of the World's Columbian Exposition. Chicago: Hayes & Co., 1892.

Flinn, John J., comp. *The Best Things to be Seen at the World's Fair.* Chicago: Columbian Guide Company, 1893.

_____. *The Official Guide to the World's Columbian Exposition in the City of Chicago: May 1–October 26, 1893.* Issued under authority of World's Columbian Exposition, Souvenir ed. Chicago: Columbian Guide Company, 1893.

Gage, Lyman J. *The World's Columbian Exposition First Annual Report of the President.* Chicago: Knight & Leonard, 1891.

Gems of the Fair. What to See and How to Find It. Chicago: World's Fair & Chicago Guide Co., n.d.

Hales, Peter Bacon. *Silver Cites: The Photography of American Urbanization 1839–1915.* Philadelphia: Temple University Press, 1984.

Hibbler, Harold E., and Charles V. Kappen. *So-Called Coins.* New York: The Coin and Currency Institute, Inc., 1963.

Johnson, Rossiter, ed. *A History of the World's Columbian Exposition Held in Chicago in 1893 by Authority of the Board of Directors.* New York: D. Appleton and Co., 1897.

Letter of Christopher Columbus to Rafael Sanchez. Facsimile of the first publication concerning America, published at Barcelona, May 1493. Chicago: The W. H. Lowdermilk Co., 1893.

Lossing, Benson J., LL.D. *1492 Columbus—America 1892. The Progress of Four Hundred Years.* New York: Gay Brothers, 1892.

Newton, Norman T. *Design on the Land. The Development of Landscape Architecture.* Cambridge, Mass.: The Belknap Press of Harvard University Press, 1971.

Official Souvenir Program of the New York Columbian Celebration October 8th to 13th 1892. New York: Rogers & Sherwood, Publishers/Printers, 1892.

Pierce, James Wilson, D.D., LL.D. *Photographic History of World's Fair.* Philadelphia; Columbus, Ohio; Toronto, Ont.: C.R. Parish & Co., 1893.

Popular Portfolio of the World's Columbian Exposition and Principal Places of Amusement. Illustrated by C. Graham. Chicago: Book Department of Seigal, Cooper & Co., 1893.

Popular Portfolios of the World's Columbian Exposition 1893. Illustrated by C. Graham. Chicago: Winter's Art Lithographing Co., 1893.

Ralph, Julian. *Chicago and the World's Fair.* New York: Harper & Brothers Publishers, 1893.

Rossen, Howard M., and John M. Kaduck. *Columbian World's Fair Collectibles, Chicago (1892-1893).* Des Moines: Wallace-Homestead Book Co., 1976.

View Album of Chicago. Columbus, Ohio: Ward Brothers, 1892.

Weimann, Jeanne Madeline. "A Dream for the 'Age of Discovery.' A Woman's Building at Chicago 1992." *World's Fair* 2, no. 3 (Summer 1982).

The White City by Lake Michigan. New York and Chicago: Witteman, 1893.

The White City Artfolio—Educational Fine Art Series 1, series 1 (March 10, 1894): Plates 1-80. Photography by W. H. Jackson. Text by Stanley Wood.

Wilkinson, Burke. *Uncommon Clay: The Life and Works of Augustus Saint Gaudens.* New York and San Diego: Harcourt Brace Jovanovich, 1895.

The World's Fair Numbers of the Cosmopolitan. Bound issues of *The Cosmopolitan Illustrated Monthly Magazine* (September 1893): 515-640 and vol. 16, no. 2 (December 1893): 129-256.

The World's Columbian Exposition. Chicago: Knight & Leonard Co., printers, 1891.

World's Columbian Exposition Illustrated 3, no. 2 (April 1893).

World's Columbian Exposition Illustrated 3, no. 4 (June 1893).

Index

Detailed map of fairgrounds on pages 48–49

Page numbers in *italic* refer to photographs and illustrations

Photo Credits